THE DROPPING OF THE ATOMIC BOMBS

THE DROPPING OF THE ATOMIC BOMBS

Essential Library

An Imprint of Abdo Publishing
abdopublishing.com

ESSENTIAL LIBRARY OF
WORLD WAR II

BY MARY MEINKING

CONTENT CONSULTANT

ALLAN M. WINKLER
DISTINGUISHED PROFESSOR OF HISTORY
MIAMI UNIVERSITY

5 0503 01107082 0

abdopublishing.com

Published by Abdo Publishing, a division of ABDO, PO Box 398166, Minneapolis, Minnesota 55439. Copyright © 2016 by Abdo Consulting Group, Inc. International copyrights reserved in all countries. No part of this book may be reproduced in any form without written permission from the publisher. Essential Library™ is a trademark and logo of Abdo Publishing.

Printed in the United States of America, North Mankato, Minnesota

052015
092015

THIS BOOK CONTAINS
RECYCLED MATERIALS

Cover Photo: Stanley Troutman/AP Images
Interior Photos: Stanley Troutman/AP Images, 1, 3; AP Images, 6, 17, 23, 25, 36, 38, 45, 52, 84, 89, 98 (right), 99 (top); Shutterstock Images, 9, 21; Los Alamos Laboratory/AP Images, 11, 32; Red Line Editorial, 14, 47, 57; Bettmann/Corbis, 18, 28, 30, 43, 46, 55, 91, 98 (left); Library of Congress, 39, 40; US Army/Library of Congress, 49, 69; Max Desfor/AP Images, 50; Corbis, 60, 75; SuperStock/Corbis, 65; APN Photo/AP Images, 66; Kingendai/AFLO/Nippon News/Corbis, 67, 83; US Army Corps of Engineers/AP Images, 70; Hulton-Deutsch Collection/Corbis, 72; US Air Force/National Museum of the US Air Force, 77; US Army A.A.F., 81, 99 (bottom); Matty Zimmerman/AP Photo, 87; HO/AP Images, 94; Hasan Sarbakhshian/AP Images, 97

Editor: Karen Latchana Kenney
Series Designers: Kelsey Oseid and Maggie Villaume

Library of Congress Control Number: 2015930969

Cataloging-in-Publication Data

Meinking, Mary.
 The dropping of the atomic bombs / Mary Meinking.
   p. cm. -- (Essential library of World War II)
Includes bibliographical references and index.
ISBN 978-1-62403-793-1
1. Hiroshima-shi (Japan)--History--Bombardment, 1945--Juvenile literature.
2. Atomic bomb--History--20th century--Juvenile literature. 3. Manhattan Project (U.S.)--History--Juvenile literature. 4. World War, 1939-1945--Japan--Juvenile literature. I. Title.
940.54--dc23

                                              2015930969

CONTENTS

Workers raised the Trinity test bomb up the steel tower in July 1945.

CHAPTER
★ 1 ★

THE TRINITY TEST

In the desolate New Mexico desert stood a tall steel tower. Perched on its top was a huge metal ball covered with wires going in every direction. Searchlight beams lit the tower, but no one was in sight.

At 5:29 a.m. on July 16, 1945, a radio announcer's voice boomed through the area, "It is now zero minus twenty minutes."[1] It was nearly time to test the most destructive weapon that had ever been made.

A BOMB TO END THE WAR

It had taken many months of development before the weapon could be tested. From May through November 1944, Dr. J. Robert Oppenheimer fought to field-test a new weapon—the plutonium atomic bomb. Oppenheimer was the director of the Los Alamos Scientific Laboratory in New Mexico, where the bomb was developed. But General Leslie Groves, the head of the Manhattan

THE FISSION PROCESS

Fission is a reaction that happens when a neutron strikes an atom, causing the atom to split. This releases more neutrons. The process continues to multiply as more atoms split, causing a chain reaction that releases energy. If enough atoms split, the chain reaction provides the energy needed to create an atomic explosion.

Project, disagreed. The Manhattan Project was the code name for the research project that produced the atomic bombs. Groves believed the United States couldn't afford to waste any plutonium on a test.

Oppenheimer and his scientific team knew the process of fission inside the plutonium bomb should work in theory. Now they needed to actually test the weapon, nicknamed the "gadget." The gadget's explosives were designed to fire at the same moment to create the chain reaction caused by fission, which in turn would set off an explosion.

There was so much riding on this bomb. President Franklin D. Roosevelt and US military leaders believed it could end World War II (1939–1945). Oppenheimer knew the bomb needed to be tested. In November 1944, Groves finally gave in.

FINDING A TEST SITE

To keep the gadget a secret, the Manhattan Project's scientists and military staff needed to find a remote location where no one could witness the test, code-named Trinity. They considered eight possible locations—from Southern California to the Gulf Coast of Texas. In May 1944, Oppenheimer, physicist Kenneth Bainbridge, and US Army officers set off to find a New Mexico location. For three days, they drove around the desert looking for a flat, desolate location.

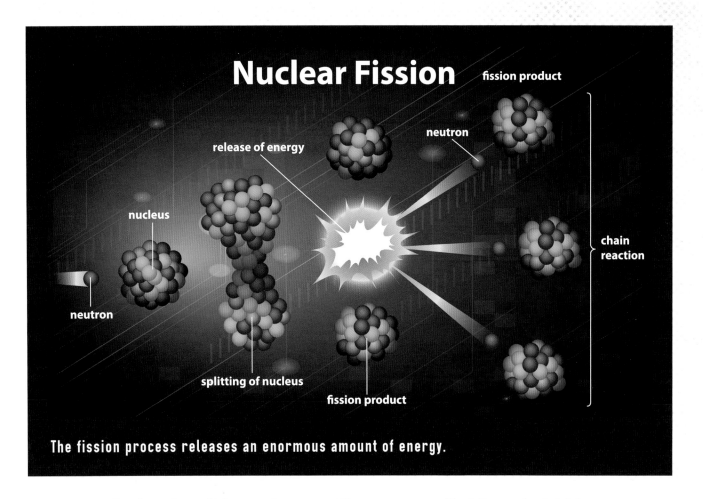

Nuclear Fission

fission product

neutron

release of energy

nucleus

neutron

chain reaction

splitting of nucleus

fission product

The fission process releases an enormous amount of energy.

Finally they found the perfect site. The area was called Jornada del Muerto in Spanish, or the "Journey of Death." It was 210 miles (338 km) south of Los Alamos. The spot was within a few hours' drive of Los Alamos, yet far enough away to keep the top-secret laboratory from being linked to a possible explosion. The government didn't want any news to get out that the United States was testing a bomb. The Los Alamos site was on the border of the US military's Alamogordo Bombing and Gunnery Range.

WORLD WAR II AND THE BOMB

The United States and its allies, including the United Kingdom, France, the Soviet Union, and China, were at war against the Axis powers of Germany and Japan. The Axis powers had dreams of world domination. Something had to be done to stop them and end the worldwide war, which began in 1939.

The Germans were close to mastering nuclear fission in atomic bombs. In response, the United States spent billions of dollars, employed a huge workforce, and found the greatest scientific geniuses to create the atomic bomb first.

On April 30, 1945, German dictator Adolf Hitler committed suicide as Allied troops closed in. His suicide ended World War II on the European front. The Japanese continued battling, though. The United States decided to use the atomic bomb on Japan, in hopes of shocking the country into surrender.

Bainbridge's job was to prepare the site for the test. Starting in February 1945, he and his staff of 25 laborers worked toward their July 4 target test date.[2] The US Army transformed a house on the site into a field laboratory.

The staff grew to more than 250 workers, many of whom were soldiers.[3] The US Army Corps of Engineers built three dirt-covered bunkers with concrete slab roofs. They were 10,000 yards (9,100 m) from Ground Zero, where the bomb would explode. Each bunker was named after its direction and distance in yards from Ground Zero. Bunker N-10,000 to the north housed recording instruments and searchlights. Bunker W-10,000 to the west housed banks of high-speed cameras and searchlights. And bunker S-10,000 to the south served as the command center. Another 5 miles (8 km) to the south was the base camp. It had the workers' tents and barracks.

The laborers built a steel tower at Ground Zero. They poured four concrete footings into the sand. They built the legs from prefabricated steel that had

The atomic bomb was developed inside the Los Alamos Laboratory in New Mexico.

been shipped to the site. The finished tower was 100 feet (30.5 m) tall with an oak platform on top. A small three-sided corrugated iron shack sat at the top to house the bomb. A heavy-duty electric winch, a lifting device, could pull the bomb up and through the removable floor of the shack.

More than 500 miles (800 km) of wires radiated from the bomb to instruments inside designated bunkers. Some wires hung from T-shaped wooden poles that were 6 feet (1.8 m) tall, while others ran through garden hoses buried underground.

CONSTRUCTION WORKERS

The men who worked on the Trinity site labored around the clock to get the job done. The daytime desert temperatures reached more than 100 degrees Fahrenheit (38°C). Every morning, the men made sure to shake their boots out, in case a scorpion, centipede, rattlesnake, or fire ant was inside. They could take only cold showers in the gypsum-tainted well water. The chalky water made their hair stiff. If they drank the water, it made them sick.

BUILDING THE GADGET

At the Los Alamos laboratory, tension was building. Harry S. Truman, who became US president when Franklin Roosevelt died on April 12, 1945, was scheduled to attend the Potsdam Conference. It was being held outside Berlin, Germany, from July 15 to August 2, 1945. World leaders gathered to negotiate terms for the end of the war. Truman wanted the Trinity test to happen during that conference, so that he could inform British prime minister Winston Churchill and Soviet leader Joseph Stalin.

Oppenheimer felt the pressure more than anyone. He and his team were building the gadget as fast as possible. But a new crisis came up every day with the complex device. His team worked through many nights to complete the project. The team worked on two bombs: one was uranium-based and the other was plutonium-based. Both used fission to create the nuclear explosion.

Inside the uranium gadget, a gun-firing mechanism would shoot one piece of U-235 uranium at another piece. But U-235 is a very rare element in nature. It took almost one year for scientists to separate the atoms of U-235 from the more common U-238 atoms to make one bomb.

The other type of gadget used man-made radioactive plutonium as its fuel. But a gun-firing mechanism wouldn't work to start the plutonium reaction. After months of experimentation, the Los Alamos scientists decided to use implosion to fire the plutonium bomb. A orange-sized ball, or core, of plutonium had explosives surrounding it. When the explosives went off, they would blast the plutonium together, creating a chain reaction that could cause an atomic explosion. The scientists had plenty of plutonium for a test bomb.

SETTING UP THE BOMB

On July 12, the plutonium core was removed from the Los Alamos vault. At approximately 6:00 p.m., the core arrived at the Trinity test site ranch house for the night. The giant implosion explosive casting, or shell, consisting of the melted and cooled explosive material in its container, left Los Alamos on July 13 at 12:01 a.m. for an eight-hour trip to the test site. A room inside the ranch house was converted into a clean room. It was thoroughly vacuumed and the windows were sealed with black electrical tape. Early in the morning on July 13, the assembly team gathered around the bomb components spread out on a table. They put together the plutonium core and packaged it for its trip to Ground Zero.

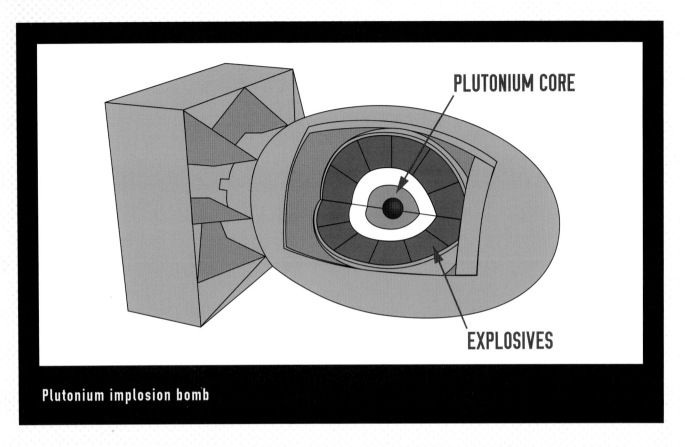

PLUTONIUM CORE

EXPLOSIVES

Plutonium implosion bomb

The truck carrying the five-foot- (1.5 m) wide explosive shell backed under the tower at Ground Zero. The five-short-ton (4.5 metric ton) bomb was slowly lifted up the tower by the winch. US Army staff piled cotton mattresses under the bomb to cushion it if it slipped from the winch. The tower's trapdoor opened and the bomb was swung into position.

WATCHING THE TEST

General Groves and other dignitaries flew into Albuquerque, New Mexico, on July 14. Almost a day later, the officials filled the bunkers and shallow trenches at the base camp, waiting for the test. Three busloads of close to 90 scientists from Los Alamos arrived at the viewing site at Compañia Hill, 20 miles (32 km) northwest of Ground Zero. Many were nervous the gadget might not work.

Among the observers was one reporter, William Laurence, from the *New York Times*. He was under strict orders from General Groves not to publish anything until given the okay to do so. Laurence wondered how he would report on anything happening so far away. A nearby scientist said, "Don't worry, you'll see all you need to."[4]

The scientists could plan and control everything except the weather. The test meteorologist, Jack Hubbard, predicted a tropical air mass would hover over the area from July 10 to July 16. The cameramen on the ground and in the air needed clear visibility. The rain could also pour down dangerous radioactive fallout after the explosion. General Groves did not want delays, so the test was set for 2:00 a.m. on July 16. But around 2:00 a.m., as predicted, thunderstorms pounded Ground Zero. They needed to push the test back

A BUBBLE PROBLEM

George Kistiakowsky was the scientist in charge of making the gadget's explosives, which surrounded the plutonium core. The shells were X-rayed on July 2. When the X ray films were held up to the light, they were dotted with black spots. These were air bubbles. Those air holes could affect the timing and the reaction of the explosion. But there was no time to recast the molds.

On July 9, a week before the Trinity test, Kistiakowsky borrowed a dental drill. All night he drilled holes to reach the air bubbles. He then filled the cavities with molten explosives. He took on this dangerous job himself to avoid endangering his staff. Kistiakowsky said, "I mean if fifty pounds [23 kg] of explosives goes off in your lap, you won't know it."[5]

a couple of hours. The rain moved on and the stars shone at Ground Zero. A 5:30 a.m. shot time was set.

At 5:09 a.m., Bainbridge unlocked the master switches, which began the 20-minute countdown. He and the remaining scientists at Ground Zero hurried to the S-10,000 control bunker, where Oppenheimer and other head scientists waited.

Groves jumped into his jeep and headed to the base camp bunker. Waiting in the total darkness, the men applied sunscreen to their faces and arms. At 5:25 a.m., a green rocket flare marked five minutes until detonation. A short siren wail from the base camp followed. Observers were instructed to lie on the ground with their feet toward Ground Zero and their arms over their heads. Others hunkered down in their bunkers or assigned locations. A long siren signaled the two-minute mark. Then the one-minute warning rocket fired at 5:29 a.m. The observers grabbed pieces of tinted welder's glass and held them to their eyes as protection against the coming bright flash. A hush fell over the crowd.

Radio announcer Sam Allison counted down. Then a blinding flash of light filled the sky. As it faded, a huge ball of fire grew from the test site. It twisted and stretched skyward into a column of changing colors. The searing heat, like that of an open oven door, accompanied the flash. The atomic bomb test was a resounding success. But would this weapon be the key to ending war?

A mushroom cloud formed during the bomb's explosion on July 16, 1945.

Professor Leo Szilard worked on atomic fission theory in the 1930s.

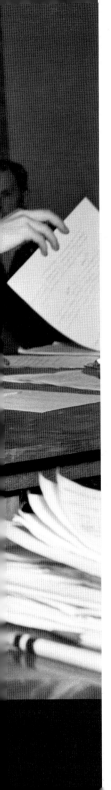

CHAPTER

★ **2** ★

BUILDING THE BOMBS

Hungarian physicist Leo Szilard formed the theory of atomic fission as early as 1933. In 1938, German chemists experimented with fission. They discovered that bombarding uranium with neutrons produced a chain reaction. Normally this was a slow process that simply created heat. But splitting a large lump of uranium atoms quickly to release energy at the same time could create a powerful bomb. News spread to the United States at the Washington Conference on Theoretical Physics in January 1939.

US scientists became increasingly concerned about Nazi Germany acquiring large quantities of uranium. If they had enough, the Germans could build an atomic bomb. The US scientists felt the need to alert President Roosevelt to stop the Germans.

In 1937, Szilard came to the United States to escape Nazi persecution and teach physics. On July 16, 1939, Szilard and fellow Hungarian physicist Eugene Wigner visited scientist Albert

Einstein. They asked him to write Roosevelt to explain that fission was possible and Germany was stockpiling uranium. Einstein, who had done theoretical work linking energy and matter, was the most famous scientist in the world. He would be the one scientist Roosevelt would listen to.

Instead of mailing Einstein's letter, Roosevelt's campaign economics writer Alexander Sachs delivered it by hand on October 11. They discussed fission, and Roosevelt said, "Alex, what you are after is to see that the Nazis don't blow us up." "Precisely," Sachs said. "This requires action," Roosevelt said.[1]

EXAMINING FISSION'S POTENTIAL

Sachs discussed fission with Dr. Lyman Briggs, who was the director of the Bureau of Standards. This government department was the nation's physics laboratory. On October 21, 1939, Briggs headed the first meeting of the Advisory Committee on Uranium. Nine leading physicists and members of the US Army and Navy discussed the potential power of a fission bomb. They also discussed the costs and materials needed to build a bomb.

The committee report to the president on November 1 stated it was worth exploring controlled fission chain reactions. The report suggested using $33,000 worth of graphite to absorb neutrons and 50 short tons (45 metric tons) of uranium oxide.[2] Roosevelt kept the report on file, but took no immediate action.

But the physicists didn't give up. Independent fission studies began around the country. The scientists knew uranium was the largest atom in nature. It had 92 protons and 143 neutrons, which totaled 235 to make U-235. The uranium isotope U-238 had 92 protons and 146 neutrons, which totaled 238. This common uranium isotope wasn't fissionable for a bomb. U-235 was the isotope

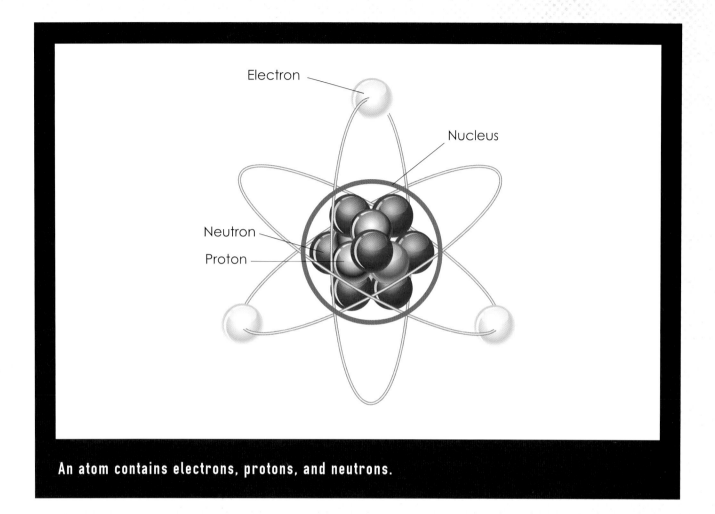

Electron

Nucleus

Neutron

Proton

they needed, but it was found in only seven out of 1,000 uranium atoms.[3] The key to making a bomb was finding a way to separate the uranium. Scientists devised different processes, but none were fast. They also experimented with different ways to control a chain reaction using heavy water or graphite.

THE ATOMIC RACE BEGINS

In June 1942, the US government got involved. President Roosevelt authorized the development and building of an atomic bomb. The US Army Corps of Engineers, headquartered in New York City, headed the plant construction. The Office of Scientific Research and Development would direct nuclear research. The project's code name was the Manhattan Project, since most of its engineers worked in Manhattan.

General Groves was in charge of the project. By September 18, he had purchased 1,200 short tons (1,090 metric tons) of high-grade uranium ore from the Belgian Congo.[4] The next day, he ordered the purchase of Site X in Oak Ridge, Tennessee, to start separating the uranium. Later that month, he toured several laboratories across the country where scientists were working on uranium atom separation and getting the kind of uranium the Manhattan Project needed.

On October 8, General Groves visited the University of California at Berkeley and met J. Robert Oppenheimer, who taught there. The men agreed that scientists should work together in a new central lab to solve the fission equation before the Germans. Groves hired Oppenheimer on October 19 as scientific director of the Manhattan Project. In time, the project research took place in more than 30 US states, the United Kingdom, and Canada, becoming one of the most expensive projects in the history of the world.

FIRST NUCLEAR CHAIN REACTION

In Chicago, Illinois, a group of physicists worked on an atomic chain reaction program at the Metallurgical Laboratory. Located under the University of

J. ROBERT OPPENHEIMER

1904–1967

Julius Robert Oppenheimer was born in New York City in 1904 to wealthy parents. Oppenheimer had an early interest in science and graduated from Harvard University in 1925 with a chemistry degree. He continued studying and achieved his doctorate in physics. He then worked at the University of California, Berkeley, in the theoretical physics department.

In October 1942, Oppenheimer became the scientific director of the Manhattan Project. He led the team of international scientists to build the first atomic bomb. On October 16, 1945, Oppenheimer resigned as the scientific director of the Manhattan Project.

He remained active in nuclear affairs and spoke out against the hydrogen bomb to the Atomic Energy Commission (AEC). AEC chairman Lewis Strauss tried to discredit Oppenheimer though. In 1954, after a long and painful hearing, Oppenheimer lost his security clearance to view atomic research. He later contracted throat cancer and died on February 18, 1967, in Princeton, New Jersey.

Chicago's football stadium was a pile of graphite bricks 25 feet (7.6 m) wide by 20 feet (6.1 m) tall. Many of the bricks in the center of the pile had holes filled with uranium cylinders. Long wooden rods covered with cadmium came out from the pile. The scientists used the rods to absorb loose neutrons, which controlled the chain reaction. Buckets of a cadmium nitrate solution were also on hand to dump on the pile to prevent the chain reaction from getting out of control.

Italian scientist Enrico Fermi was in charge of the experiment on December 2, 1942. Other scientists and students joined Fermi on a balcony overlooking the pile. Scientific machines counted flying neutrons by making clicking sounds. Fermi ordered that the first cadmium rod be removed to start the chain reaction. He did some quick calculations and ordered the second rod removed. This continued until only the last control rod remained to hold the reaction in check.

Fermi instructed George Weil to pull the rod halfway out. Then Weil continued to pull the rod out at intervals until it was totally removed. The machines roared as they counted neutrons while the nuclear chain reaction occurred. Fermi let it go on for four and a half minutes and then ordered that the rod be reinserted.

LIKE BURNING TRASH

The first atomic chain reaction, called the Chicago Pile-1, took place under the football stadium at the University of Chicago. To simplify what happened during fission, Fermi compared it to a burning pile of trash.

Fermi said, "An atomic chain reaction may be compared to the burning of a rubbish pile from spontaneous combustion. In such a fire, minute parts of the pile start to burn and in turn ignite other tiny fragments. When sufficient numbers of these fractional parts are heated to the kindling points, the entire heap bursts into flames."[5]

Enrico Fermi began experimenting with uranium in the 1930s in Italy.

The clicking slowly subsided. The first controlled nuclear chain reaction had been a success.

LOS ALAMOS

Now that researchers knew a nuclear chain reaction would work, the Manhattan Project needed a remote location where the atomic bomb research could be done in secret. This location needed to be close to railroad lines to transport people and supplies. On November 16, Oppenheimer and Groves found the Los Alamos Ranch School in the mountains of northern New Mexico. It was just what they were looking for. It already had a few buildings in a remote location. The school's

SITE X

Three plants at Site X in Oak Ridge, Tennessee, separated uranium using different methods. Plant Y-12 used electromagnetic separation. This process uses giant magnets to separate the two types of uranium in a two-step process. It vaporized the uranium to collect the lighter U-235, which was approximately 90 percent pure.[6]

The second plant, K-25, used a process called gaseous diffusion to enrich the uranium. In this process, the uranium is converted into a gas and then pumped through a series of screenlike barrier tubes.

The lighter U-235 goes through the barrier tubes, while the heavier U-238 cannot.

The third plant, S-50, used liquid thermal diffusion. In this process, vertical pipes were cooled on the outside and heated on the inside by steam. The U-235 stayed closer to the heat and rose more quickly than the U-238.

The first shipment of U-235 was sent to Los Alamos in early March 1944. By the summer of 1945, Site X had produced enough U-235 to fuel one atomic bomb.

director soon received a letter from US Secretary of War Henry Stimson stating that the school's property was needed for military purposes. The school was closed and construction of the Los Alamos Laboratory began. It came to be known as Site Y.

Oppenheimer gathered the best scientific minds in the United States who were working with atomic energy. The scientists began arriving in March 1943, but they didn't know what they'd be working on.

On April 15, Oppenheimer's assistant, Robert Serber, opened the introductory meeting at the laboratory, where approximately 40 physicists had gathered. Serber said, "The object of the project is to produce a practical military weapon in the form of a bomb in which the energy is released by a fast-neutron chain reaction."[7]

Over the next few weeks, the physicists began building an atomic bomb. Using Fermi's chain reaction success, they needed to scale down a reaction to make a bomb small enough to drop from an airplane. The scientists also needed to create a faster chain reaction to cause the huge explosion needed for a weapon.

The scientists concluded the best way to quickly start the chain reaction was to use a gun-firing mechanism to fire one piece of U-235 uranium at another piece. They housed this mechanism inside a long bomb assembly body that they nicknamed Little Boy.

In the meantime, scientists discovered that when the common U-238 was hit with flying neutrons, it absorbed the neutrons instead of splitting. This made a new element—plutonium—that could also make a nuclear chain reaction. But the gun-firing mechanism wasn't fast enough for plutonium.

Atomic scientists, *left to right*: Kenneth Bainbridge, Joseph Hoffman, J. Robert Oppenheimer, L. H. Hempelman, R. F. Bacher, V. W. Weisskopf, and Richard W. Dodson

The Los Alamos scientists decided to use a shell of explosives around the plutonium core. The explosives would implode upon and compress the core, creating an atomic explosion. A ball of plutonium was packed inside the explosive shell, which was housed inside a long, round bomb assembly body nicknamed Fat Man.

SITE W'S PLUTONIUM

Scientists found that plutonium undergoes fission more quickly than U-235, making it useful for atomic bombs. Plutonium was first made at Site X in 1943.

A new location with plenty of water for cooling was needed to produce the plutonium, and Hanford, Washington, soon became Site W. It was based on the Oak Ridge cooling reactor but on a much larger scale. Uranium was exposed to radiation, creating plutonium, which was then pushed into a pool of water for 60 days. The first plutonium began arriving in Los Alamos in the summer of 1944.

The Fat Man—type bomb was used for the Trinity test.

TESTING THE BOMB

The plutonium Fat Man atomic bomb was built, but scientists needed to test it. Groves wanted to contain the expensive plutonium to use again. Oppenheimer and Groves agreed they should try to contain the possible radioactive bomb fragments.

They considered a possible container, a gigantic steel tank shaped like a trash can, but then scientists feared that testing the gadget inside the tank would alter their measurements. In the end, they opted instead for a test out in the open—at Trinity.

COPY BOMB

A few days before the Trinity test, Oppenheimer insisted on testing the implosion part of the gadget. A copy bomb with high explosives was the same as the Trinity bomb, except it didn't have a plutonium core. The explosive shell for the Trinity test had to be perfect, with

no chips, cracks, or other imperfections. The rejected explosives were given to the group building the copy.

Physicist Edward Creutz was in charge of testing the copy to make sure all the explosives fired at the same time. However, the test failed and the explosives didn't all fire together. Creutz called Oppenheimer and told him the bad news. He thought the Trinity bomb was likely to fail.

The Trinity test was going to take place as scheduled. Groves and the arriving dignitaries expected a demonstration of the most powerful weapon ever built. But after the copy's implosion failure, everyone was on edge. There was no time to fix the bomb before the Trinity test.

The bomb exploded from the top of the 100-foot- (30 m) tall testing tower.

A BLINDING SUCCESS

At 5:29 a.m., July 16, 1945, the automatic timer counted down to zero. This remotely triggered the explosives inside the Fat Man bomb perched atop the Trinity tower. The shell exploded inward, compressing the plutonium and creating a chain reaction. The result was a nuclear explosion. Despite doubts, the bomb had worked. The scientists and local residents witnessed history that early morning. The director of Trinity, Kenneth Bainbridge, said, "No one who saw it could forget it, a foul and awesome display."[1]

Witnesses peering through welder's glass during the Trinity blast saw the horizon light up with a flash many times brighter than the midday sun. The giant white fireball changed to yellow and then orange. The ball started to rise and billow and then turned black around the edges. *New York Times* reporter Laurence later wrote, "A great ball of fire about a mile in diameter, changing colors as it kept shooting upward, from deep purple to orange, expanding, growing bigger, rising as it expanded."[2]

A hush fell over the crowd, as people watched the brilliant blast. Light travels faster than sound, so the silence was broken a full 30 seconds later with an

RADIATION POISONING

Radiation is a form of energy that occurs naturally, but it can harm people when they are exposed to too much of it. Both types of atomic bombs emitted high levels of radiation during the fission process. The odorless, tasteless, invisible radiation of atomic blasts has enough energy to damage the DNA in people's cells.

High doses of radiation can cause people to develop fevers and vomit blood. Radiation can also cause various types of cancer such as leukemia, thyroid cancer, and breast cancer. It can also cause birth defects.

BOMB POOL

The scientists started a pool with their guesses on how large the explosion would be. They each bet one dollar on the explosive yield of the Trinity blast. The bets ranged from 45,000 short tons (40,800 metric tons) to zero tons of TNT. Kistiakowsky picked 1,400 short tons (1,270 metric tons) and Oppenheimer picked 300 short tons (270 metric tons). Isidor Rabi took the last spot left in the pool and picked 18,000 short tons (16,300 metric tons). From the debris collected, the actual explosive yield was 18,600 short tons (16,870 metric tons) of TNT.[4] It was nearly four times what the Los Alamos scientists estimated it would be. Rabi won the pool.

enormous boom. A loud rumble followed and it echoed back and forth between the mountains. The heat of the bomb hit the observers' faces and hands. Many, even those ten miles (16 km) away, said they could feel the heat.

Kistiakowsky, standing at S-10,000, was knocked down by the blast but scrambled to his feet to watch the fireball rise. Oppenheimer said, "We knew the world would not be the same. A few people laughed, a few people cried. Most were silent."[3]

CIVILIANS' REACTIONS

The explosion was heard up to 150 miles (240 km) away in El Paso, Texas. The shock wave rattled windows up to 200 miles (320 km) away in Silver City, New Mexico. And people saw the flash as far as 450 miles (720 km) away in Amarillo, Texas.

Stories about the blast varied—from people getting knocked out of bed to roosters crowing early to a blind girl sensing the blast. Residents from miles around noticed a white powder that fell on everything, like an early frost. People called their local police, newspapers, and radio stations looking for answers. Was it an earthquake, a meteor, an airplane crash, the Japanese attacking, or a massive fireworks show?

A statement to be sent to newspapers after the blast had been prepared two weeks before the Trinity test. The cover-up story stated, "Several inquiries have been received concerning a heavy explosion which occurred on the Alamogordo Air Base reservation this morning. A remotely located ammunition magazine containing a considerable amount of high explosives and pyrotechnics exploded. There was no loss of life or injury to anyone."[5]

WHAT REMAINED

Later on the morning of July 16, physicist Herbert Anderson and others rode to Ground Zero in a lead-lined tank to protect them from the radiation. From the periscope, they could see the giant crater left behind from the explosion. It measured six feet (1.8 m) deep and had a 1,200-foot (370 m) diameter. The

GREEN GLASS

The heat from the Trinity blast fused the desert's sand into green glass that covered an area of more than 1,200 feet (370 m) radiating from Ground Zero. The sand fused into various shapes and sizes, creating the mineral trinitite. Some pieces of trinitite had spots of black, blue, or red. These colors probably came from metals in the tower or bomb wires that were vaporized during the explosion.

On September 9, 1945, Groves invited newsmen and scientists to Trinity to write about the test. Many of the newsmen picked up pieces of trinitite as souvenirs. Local hotels and banks gave away or sold the trinitite to tourists, and jewelry was made from the green mineral. Tourists were unaware the trinitite was radioactive. In 1952, most remaining trinitite was removed or buried to clean up the site. It is now a federal crime to remove trinitite from the area.

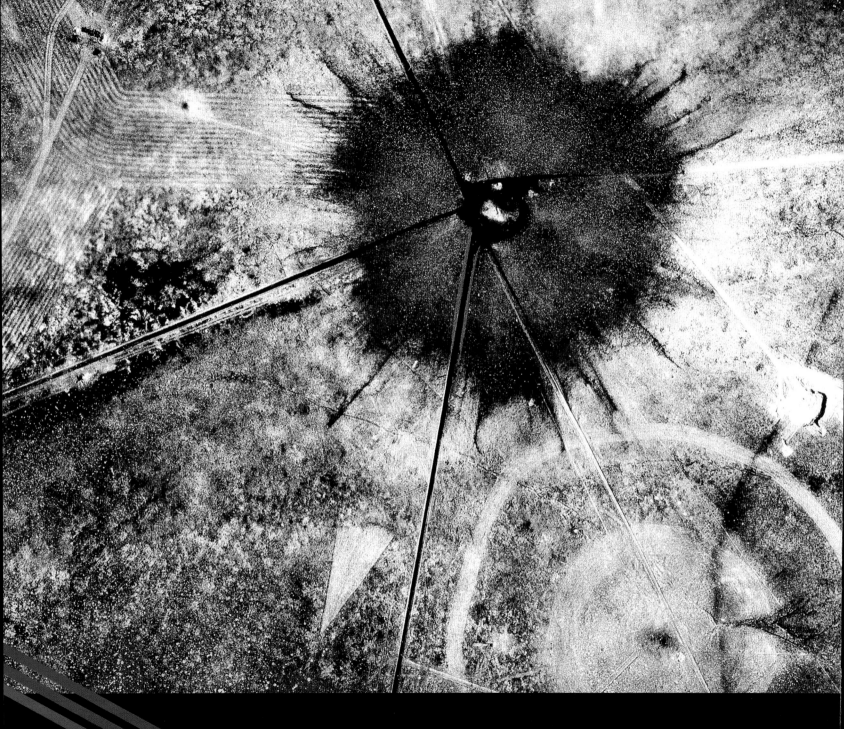

An aerial view shows the large crater caused by the Trinity test explosion.

tower, winch, wooden platform, and steel girders were all gone. Everything was vaporized except the twisted wreckage of the tower's footings. At Ground Zero, the fireball had reached 14,710 degrees Fahrenheit (8,150°C). That is approximately four times the temperature of the center of the sun.[6]

Animals in the area during the blast died instantly or were badly burned or blinded. Frogs, jackrabbits, lizards, and snakes were annihilated. Plants were uprooted, blown over, or vaporized to dust.

MAKING THE DECISION

Everyone involved with the Manhattan Project believed they were building the atomic bombs to drop them on Germany. But on April 30, 1945, German leader Adolf Hitler committed suicide as the Soviets approached Berlin. On May 8, the Germans surrendered. German troops laid down their arms, and victory was declared in Europe. But the war was only halfway over. A battle still raged with Japan. US bombers attacked Japan every night. On March 9, 1945, a B-29 bombing raid over Tokyo used incendiary firebombs and killed 100,000 Japanese people.[7] It didn't look like Japan was ever going to surrender.

After President Roosevelt's death on April 12, 1945, Vice President Harry S. Truman became president. He was then let in on the biggest secret of

BABY IS BORN

With the successful bomb test at Trinity, General Groves needed to alert President Truman. Truman was in Berlin at the Potsdam Conference. Groves couldn't openly call Truman or send him a telegram. He feared the Soviets would be listening in and hear the news, too. Instead, Groves sent a coded telegram message to Washington, DC, which was forwarded to Truman. It said, "Baby is born."[8] That meant the atomic bomb test had been a success.

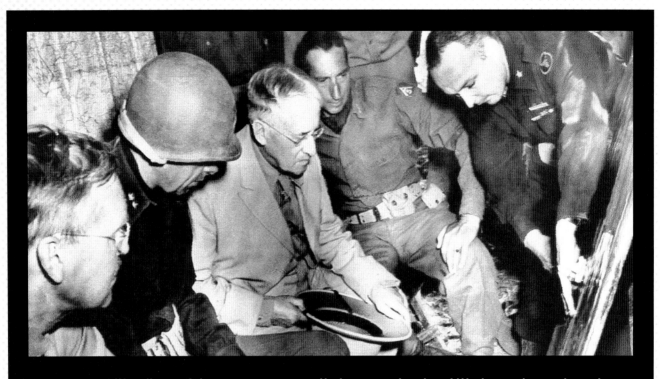

Secretary of War Henry Stimson, *center*, studied a map showing Allied attacks against the Germans in Italy on July 10, 1944.

World War II—the Manhattan Project. Truman felt he needed to continue Roosevelt's vision of using atomic bombs to end the war.

Truman appointed the Interim Committee to help him make the decision to use the bomb. Secretary of War Stimson headed the committee. Its members were scientists and politicians. After considering the facts, on June 1 the committee decided that "the bomb should be used against Japan as soon as possible, that it be used on a war plant surrounded by workers' homes; and that it be used without prior warning."[9] Truman agreed.

HARRY S. TRUMAN
1884–1972

Harry S. Truman was born on May 8, 1884, in Lamar, Missouri, to a farming family. He loved reading history books and dreamed of becoming a great soldier. After graduating from high school in 1901, Truman served in the Missouri National Guard. He served in World War I from 1917 to 1919 in the 129th Field Artillery in France. He then served as a judge for the Jackson County Court in Missouri.

In 1934, Truman was elected a US senator for Missouri. In 1944, Truman ran as vice president with Franklin D. Roosevelt and they won. Roosevelt died on April 12, 1945 and Truman was sworn in the same day as the United States' thirty-third president. That evening, Secretary of War Stimson handed Truman a memo that said, "Within four months we shall in all probability have completed the most terrible weapon ever known in human history, one bomb which could destroy a whole city."[10] Until that meeting, Truman was unaware of the Manhattan Project.

After the Trinity test, Truman approved use of the atomic bomb on Japan. Truman was reelected to a second term as president. He retired in 1953 to Independence, Missouri. Truman died on December 26, 1972.

The B-29 Superfortress was the only plane large enough to carry the atomic bombs internally.

TRAINING AND TARGETS

By August 1945, the United States had two atomic bombs in its arsenal. Little Boy was a long uranium bomb, which detonated with a gun-firing mechanism. Fat Man was the second bomb. It used plutonium and was housed in an oval container. The bombs were ready to be used, but how to transport the bombs had not yet been solved. Los Alamos physicist Norman Ramsey was in charge of finding a way to transport the atomic bombs and drop them on their targets.

The only US plane that could handle the size of the bombs was the B-29 Superfortress. These huge planes were first made in September 1943, but they had to be modified for the bombs. By November 29, the modification of the B-29s began. With the modifications, the planes could carry the Little Boy and the Fat Man bombs.

THE NORDEN BOMBSIGHT

One important secret weapon of World War II was the Norden bombsight. The US Air Force used the bombsights during daylight bombing runs. Bomber crews looked through the device, which calculated the path a bomb would take through the air, factoring in wind and other conditions. The bombsights gave the troops better accuracy than any other air force in the world. The Norden computerized bombsight ran on automatic pilot, which flew the plane and dropped the bombs over their targets. Should a plane be shot down, the bombardier was responsible for destroying the bombsight so it wouldn't fall into enemy hands.

The planes were ready, but now the United States needed to perfect the bombs and their deployment. On March 3, 1944, the first dummy bombs were dropped at the Muroc Army Air Force Base in California. The dummy bombs had no nuclear material inside. Their fuses, falling patterns, and timing were perfected during these tests, so when the armed bombs dropped there would be no question where they would land.

TRAINING PILOTS

The US Army Air Force now needed to train pilots and crews to fly the huge planes and accurately drop the bombs. By late August, Air Force Commanding General Henry "Hap" Arnold had chosen the leader of this special group of pilots. The best US bomber pilot was Lieutenant Colonel Paul W. Tibbets. He was the obvious choice to lead the other pilots, put together the crews, and deliver the new atomic weapon. In September, Tibbets became the leader of the 393rd Bombardment Squadron.

Wendover Field in Utah became the home base for the newly formed group. This isolated location was a perfect place to conduct bombing practices. By September, the pilots moved to Wendover along with a troop carrier and other support groups, who moved men and their necessary cargo. They were then

PAUL W. TIBBETS

1915–2007

Paul Warfield Tibbets Jr. was born on February 23, 1915, in Quincy, Illinois, to mother Enola Gay and father Paul Tibbets. At age 12, Paul was asked to toss candy from an airplane to the crowds at a racetrack and beach. From that day on, Paul wanted to be a pilot.

In 1937, Tibbets joined the US Army Air Corps and graduated first in his class. He flew several types of planes on missions over German-occupied Europe and North Africa to become one of the United States' best pilots. In September 1944, Tibbets became the commander of the 509th Composite Group. On August 6, 1945, Tibbets piloted the *Enola Gay* B-29 bomber plane, named after his mother. His plane dropped the first atomic bomb over Hiroshima, Japan.

Following World War II, Tibbets remained in the Air Force. He retired in 1966. He owned an air taxi company in Columbus, Ohio, until he retired in 1985. Tibbets died on November 1, 2007, at 92 years old.

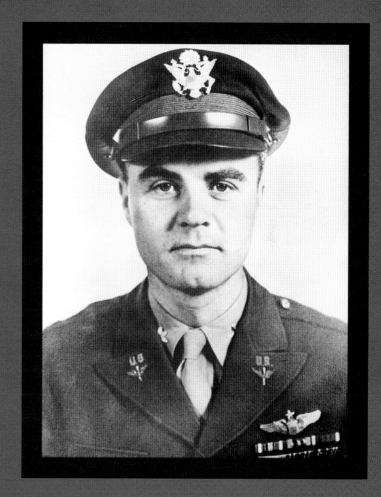

renamed the 509th Composite Group. By October, new modified B-29s began arriving at the base.

Tibbets collected the world's best pilots, bombardiers, navigators, and flight engineers he could find. More than 225 officers and 1,542 enlisted men reported to him.[1] Security was tight to prevent any leaks to enemies about the new top-secret bombing mission. Tibbets opened his men's mail, monitored their phones, and even had them followed.

Tibbets didn't tell the crew what type of bombs they'd be carrying. The bombardiers, crew who specialized in releasing bombs, practiced dropping dummy bombs from 30,000 feet (9,000 m) using their bombing sites. As they continued, the targets marking the desert floor got smaller and smaller. Tibbets told them that after a bomb was released, the pilots were to immediately nose the airplane at a sharp 155-degree daredevil diving turn. This dive increased their airspeed so the plane could get ten miles (16 km) away before the bomb exploded. The crews had no idea why this mattered, but they followed their orders.

B-29 SUPERFORTRESSES

The giant B-29 Superfortress was the first pressurized bomber ever made. A tube allowed the crew to move between its two pressurized chambers. The B-29 needed more than 8,000 feet (2,440 m) to take off. Its long polished aluminum body ended in a tail. The B-29's wingspan was the length of half a football field. And it had retractable three-wheeled landing gear. The B-29s could fly up to 365 miles per hour (587 kmh) to handle missions of 5,830 miles (9,380 km) round trip. Each plane had 30 fuel tanks that carried more than 9,400 gallons (35,580 L) of gas. The B-29s could fly at an altitude of 30,000 feet (9,000 m), which was high enough to avoid bursting shells from antiaircraft guns. The planes even had remote control guns, radar-assisted navigation, and radar-assisted bombing to help hit their targets.

Tibbets picked his best crew to send to Batista Field, Cuba, for six weeks of training. There they got experience using radar and flying over open water, so they'd be ready to fly to Japan's mainland.

THE TINIAN BASE

In early June 1945, Tibbets went to Tinian, the US-controlled island close to mainland Japan. He arrived to inspect the facilities for his crew and the B-29s. The construction crew built warehouses, buildings, roads, parking for the B-29s, pits for loading the bombs, and an air-conditioned building to assemble the bombs.

The island was transformed into the largest airport in the world. Six parallel runways stretched for two miles (3.2 km) down the island. Each was the width of a ten-lane highway.

More than 1,100 members of the 509th crew made their way to Tinian by

Tibbets piloted his plane the *Enola Gay* on the atomic bomb mission.

TINIAN AND IWO JIMA:
TWO STRATEGIC ISLANDS

The Allies wanted to attack Japan's mainland, but flights from Hawaii were too long. So the Allies needed to control neighboring Japanese islands. They could be used as bases for their attack on Japan.

The island of Tinian, part of the Mariana chain of islands, was taken on August 1, 1944, after a bloody battle. The Allies quickly converted the island into a launching point for air attacks on Japan, which was 1,500 miles (2,400 km) away.

The island of Iwo Jima was heavily entrenched with Japanese forces. But it was needed as an Allied base as it was closer to the Japanese coast. The island was secured by March 26, 1945, but US troops had approximately 28,000 casualties.[2] The island was quickly converted into a landing zone for the Allies.

The small island of Iwo Jima was an important Allied base during the war.

ship.[3] The first of Tibbets's combat crew flew to the island on June 10 in their newly modified B-29s. The planes were unarmed except for the tail gunner. These B-29s were the finest used in the war in the Pacific. By the end of June, 11 of the modified B-29s arrived at Tinian.[4]

The 509th flight crews continued their bombing run practices. They navigated to and from Iwo Jima, the Allied-controlled island stopover on the route to Japan. They dropped dummy bombs nicknamed pumpkins and general-purpose bombs.

POSSIBLE TARGET SITES

The bomb would be ready to be dropped after August 1, 1945. US officials had to choose which Japanese city they would target. The Target Committee, under General Groves, came up with a list of 17 possible target cities of more than three miles (4.8 km) in diameter.[5] Cities already destroyed by bombings would be deleted from the list. The committee focused on cities that had industries or military bases. But cities with cultural areas such as shrines would be avoided. Truman said, "Soldiers and sailors are the target and not women and children. . . . The target will be a purely military one."[6] The top three target cities chosen were Hiroshima, Kokura, and Niigata. The city of Nagasaki was later added to the list.

BRIEFING THE CREWS

At 3:00 p.m. on August 4, the seven 509th B-29 crews gathered for their briefing on the secret bombing mission for which they were training. Tibbets told the crews the weapon they were about to deliver had been successfully tested in the

An aerial view shows the target city of Hiroshima before the bomb was dropped.

The *Enola Gay* crew

United States and was going to be dropped on Japan. Two intelligence officers revealed blackboards showing maps of the three possible target cities: Hiroshima, Kokura, and Nagasaki.

Then Tibbets explained that three B-29 planes would leave before everyone else. They would fly ahead to evaluate the cloud cover over each of the three cities and report back. Two other B-29s would accompany Tibbets's plane, the *Enola Gay*, to photograph and observe. And the seventh plane would wait on Iwo Jima as a spare, in case something happened to Tibbets's plane.

Captain William Parsons explained that the bombs were the most destructive weapons in the history of warfare. He had planned to show the crews a movie of the Trinity test, but the projector didn't work, so he just described it instead. The men were stunned.

If the weather was right, Tibbets told them, the mission should take place in the early morning of August 6. He thanked the men for their service and said the raid might cut the length of the war by at least six months. He also told the men to keep the mission a complete secret.

CHUCKING PUMPKINS

A "pumpkin" was another name for the dummy Fat Man bombs dropped on practice missions by the 509th Composite Group. They were painted bright orange for easy visibility and were of the approximate size and weight of the round Fat Man bomb. Some pumpkin bombs were made of concrete and others were filled with high explosives. It took practice to get the pumpkin bombs to fall on-target. Field tests perfected the pilots' timing. Each B-29 could carry at least two pumpkins. From October 1944 to August 1945, the pilots dropped 155 pumpkin test bombs.[7]

The Little Boy bomb had a long, thin body.

CHAPTER 5

TRANSPORTING THE BOMBS

For safety reasons, an armed atomic bomb couldn't be shipped fully assembled. The bomb could also fall into the wrong hands and be used against the United States. Instead, the atomic bombs were shipped in pieces. All the bombs' parts traveled under high security and received special treatment. This shipping program went by code name The Bronx. The final work on the U-235 projectile bullet was finished on July 3, 1945.

Two days before the Trinity test, on July 14, 1945, Little Boy was ready to leave Los Alamos for Tinian. The bomb assembly body was sent separately from its active uranium parts. Three crates containing the disassembled bomb were strapped to the back of a closed black truck. One crate contained the projectile bullet for Little Boy. The second crate contained special tools and scientific instruments. The third crate contained Little Boy's unarmed bomb assembly body.

Two army officers, Captain James Nolan and Major Robert Furman, escorted the crates. Seven carloads of security guards surrounded the truck to protect it. The convoy headed to Kirtland Army Air Force Base in Albuquerque, New Mexico.

The crates and their officer escorts flew on two DC-3s from Kirtland to Hamilton Field, near San Francisco, California. The crates were put into two trucks. A security convoy escorted the trucks to a naval shipyard hangar in San Francisco's Harbor.

UNDERCOVER ARTILLERY OFFICERS

Captain James Nolan and Major Robert Furman told the ship's crew they were artillery officers. But they knew very little about artillery. When the crew asked them what kind of guns they fired, Nolan tried demonstrating the size by cupping his hands. Furman told of 2.95-inch (75 mm) guns he used in the past, in the horse-drawn artillery days. The pair looked even less official with their field artillery collar insignias upside down. In truth, Nolan was a radiation medical officer in charge of monitoring radiation coming from the Little Boy projectile bullet. And Furman was the chief of foreign intelligence for the Manhattan Project.

ABOARD THE USS *INDIANAPOLIS*

The 10,000-pound (4,500 kg) crate containing Little Boy's bomb assembly body was loaded onto the deck of the USS *Indianapolis*. It was then welded to the deck. A 39-man round-the-clock Marine guard protected the crate marked "Secret: U.S. Government."[1]

Nolan and Furman carried aboard the Little Boy projectile bullet. It was in a three-by-four-foot (0.9 by 1.2 m) bucket-shaped lead-lined canister. On board, the canister was strapped to bolts welded to the floor of a private stateroom.

The Little Boy's bomb assembly body and projectile bullet were shipped to Tinian on the USS *Indianapolis*.

Once on course, Captain Charles Butler McVay told the crew of a special evacuation plan they must follow if it was necessary to abandon the ship. The special cargo in the stateroom was to be placed in a lifeboat before anybody or anything else. A lifeboat was tied to a bulkhead near Nolan and Furman's cabin.

The USS *Indianapolis* stopped in Hawaii to refuel and resupply for the remainder of its voyage. Their ship was the only one at the Pearl Harbor docks.

Nobody without orders could leave the ship. Captain McVay was afraid members of his crew could have learned too much about their special cargo and would tell others on shore. After six hours in port, the ship headed off toward Tinian.

On the morning of July 26, the USS *Indianapolis* arrived at Tinian's harbor. The ship had made it in record time, traveling 5,000 miles (8,000 km) from San Francisco to Tinian in ten days.

A swarm of small boats carrying generals, admirals, and other high-ranking officers along with heavily armed marines greeted the ship. The officers climbed aboard and checked the canister and the large crate. The crew lowered the

USS *INDIANAPOLIS* SINKS

The USS *Indianapolis* delivered the Little Boy atomic bomb to Tinian on July 26, 1945. The ship was to join the USS *Idaho* in the Philippines to prepare for the invasion of Japan. Captain Charles McVay requested a destroyer to escort the ship across the Philippine Sea, but was denied.

At 12:14 a.m. on July 30, a Japanese submarine targeted the *Indianapolis*. Two torpedoes struck the *Indianapolis* and she sank within minutes. Very few life rafts made it into the water. The US Navy ignored the distress calls, thinking it was a trick by the Japanese. Of the 1,196 men aboard, approximately 900 made it off the ship alive.[2]

Four days later, a US bomber on a routine antisubmarine patrol spotted the men in the water. The nearby USS *Cecil Doyle* came to the rescue. By the time the men were plucked from the water, after five days of fighting sharks, only 317 men survived.[3] This was the worst naval disaster in US history.

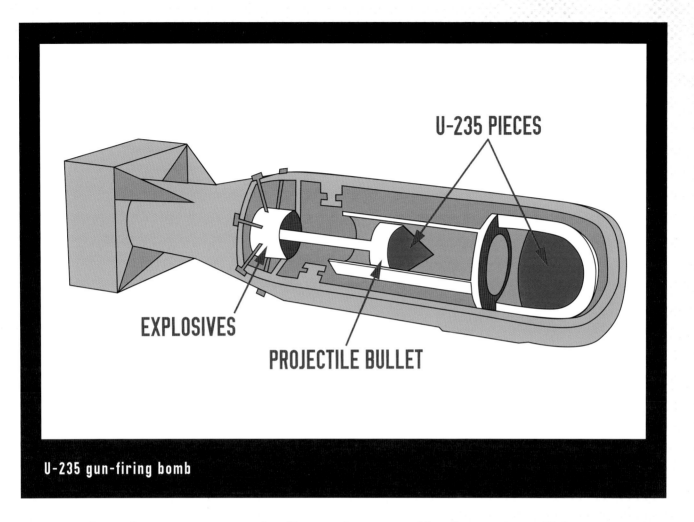

U-235 PIECES

EXPLOSIVES

PROJECTILE BULLET

U-235 gun-firing bomb

containers into two separate landing crafts manned by the marines. Nolan and Furman climbed in beside the canister, and the floating convoy sped off toward shore.

LITTLE BOY'S URANIUM

The same day the USS *Indianapolis* arrived in Tinian, on July 26, the uranium for the Little Boy bomb left Kirtland Army Air Force Base in New Mexico in three pieces. One went aboard each of the three Air Transport Command C-54 planes heading to Tinian.

The three C-54 planes refueled on the West Coast and then on Hawaii, Johnston Island, and Kwajalein before arriving on Tinian on July 28. Now all the parts were on Tinian and the Little Boy uranium bomb could be built.

LITTLE BOY AND FAT MAN[4]

Bomb	Little Boy	Fat Man
Length	10.8 feet (3.3 m)	10.8 feet (3.3 m)
Weight	9,700 pounds (4,400 kg)	10,800 pounds (4,899 kg)
Active Isotope	U-235	Plutonium
Firing Mechanism	Gun-firing	Implosion

GETTING FAT MAN THERE

Scientists at Los Alamos decided to separate Fat Man's parts for shipment, too. The plutonium core was about the size of an orange and weighed 11 pounds (5 kg). It was created as two plutonium hemispheres. Between the plutonium halves would be a small initiator made of two chemical elements, polonium and beryllium. The initiator would speed up the bomb's fission chain reaction.

On July 26, two Air Transport Command C-54s at Kirtland Army Air Force Base, New Mexico, were ready to go. One carried Fat Man's plutonium core and the other carried Fat Man's initiator.

The courier for the plutonium core from Los Alamos to Tinian was Lieutenant William King, of the US Army's intelligence security division. He picked up the two- to three-foot (0.6 to 0.9 m) steel rod frame with an 8- to 12-inch (20.3 to 30.5 cm) diameter ball inside. The lead-lined ball contained the plutonium core. King called it the "birdcage" and stayed with it for the next two days of travel.[5] The planes stopped in San Francisco, Hawaii, and Johnston Island, and finally made it to Tinian on July 28.

Also on July 28, three B-29s left Kirtland with three Fat Man bomb bodies, one per plane. Inside each bomb were the implosion explosives needed for each plutonium bomb. The Fat Man bomb assembly bodies were named F-31, F-32, and F-33. They arrived on Tinian on August 2. Now the Fat Man and Little Boy bombs needed to be assembled.

The *Enola Gay* prepared for takeoff on its historic bombing mission on August 6, 1945.

DROPPING LITTLE BOY

On Sunday morning, August 5, the US Navy base in Guam reported the weather over the three target cities would clear by the following day. So the commanders agreed the mission would take place on August 6, 1945.

A loading crew put the Little Boy bomb assembly body on a transport dolly, covered it with a tarp, and wheeled it to the loading pit. They towed the *Enola Gay* beside the loading pit. The crew then turned the plane on a giant turntable to position the bomb bay over the loading pit. A hydraulic lift raised Little Boy into the plane. They taxied the *Enola Gay* to its hardstand where its final tests and preparations were completed by 6:00 p.m. Guards kept a constant watch over the plane and its contents.

At the August 6 midnight briefing, Tibbets cautioned the crew about the power of the bomb they'd be carrying. He told them to wear their protective goggles and follow their procedures.

The chaplain said a prayer, and then the men had an early breakfast. They went to the *Enola Gay*, where they were the focus of a photo session.

Tibbets walked around the *Enola Gay*, making the final checks. The crew climbed aboard to check the instruments and radio equipment. The engines fired up. Tibbets spoke with the tower to get takeoff directions, using the code name Dimples Eight Two for the *Enola Gay*. Tibbets decided he needed the entire runway to gain the speed needed to get off the ground. At 2:45 a.m., the *Enola Gay* sped down the runway and took off into the dark sky.

EN ROUTE TO JAPAN

Shortly after takeoff, Captain Parsons from Los Alamos, who was on board to arm the bomb, and Second Lieutenant Morris Jeppson, a weapons expert, entered the unpressurized, cramped bomb bay. They inserted the four sections of the gunpowder-like cordite to finish the bomb's assembly. They planned to arm the bomb when they were closer to Japan.

An automatic piloting system took over flying the plane at 5,000 feet (1,500 m), headed for Iwo Jima. At 5:52 a.m., they reached Iwo Jima and Tibbets took

WEATHER CODES

The *Enola Gay* was on strict orders to use only a visual sighting and not radar to drop the Little Boy bomb. Clear skies were very important to see their target. The three weather planes flew to their assigned destinations. The B-29 named *Straight Flush* flew to Hiroshima, *Jabbitt III* flew to Kokura, and *Full House* flew to Nagasaki. In order to keep information from the enemies, the weather reports from the three planes were sent in code.

At 8:15 a.m. on August 6, the radio operator of the *Straight Flush* tapped out the coded message "Y-3, Q-3, B-2, C-1" over Hiroshima.[1] Tibbets translated the message to find out the cloud cover was less than 30 percent at all altitudes. C-1 meant to bomb the primary target of Hiroshima.

over the controls to climb to 9,300 feet (2,800 m). Military observation and photo planes were waiting at that elevation with their scientific instruments and cameras.

At 7:30 a.m., Parsons and Jeppson climbed back into the bomb bay to arm Little Boy. They pulled out the green plugs that blocked the firing signal and prevented an accidental detonation. They put in the red plugs and activated the bomb's internal battery. Parsons told Tibbets that Little Boy was final, meaning it was armed and ready to go.

At 8:15 a.m., Tibbets heard from the weather planes that Hiroshima had less cloud cover than the other two target cities. "It's Hiroshima," he announced to the crew.[2] The two escort planes dropped back to record the event.

MIDAIR ARMING

The new B-29s were prone to crashing. The night before the Hiroshima flight of August 6, four B-29s crashed on takeoff from Tinian. Their charred frames lined the runway when the *Enola Gay* took off.

Originally, the atomic bombs were to be armed on Tinian before takeoff for Japan. But at Los Alamos two months before, there was a heated discussion between Groves, Oppenheimer, and the arming committee about arming the bomb in flight. Groves and Oppenheimer opposed it, saying it would be too easy for something to go wrong in the air. They believed it would be dangerous to perform the precise arming procedure on a vibrating plane. Also, the unheated, cramped bomb bay would have little room for two men working on the bomb. But they knew they didn't want an atomic bomb to explode on takeoff from Tinian. In the end, they decided to go with in-flight arming of the bomb.

ATOMIC DETONATION

As it approached Hiroshima, the *Enola Gay* leveled off at 31,000 feet (9,400 m). The crew pulled on their flak suits, to protect themselves from possible shrapnel, and wore dark protective goggles. They had memorized the maps and aerial photos of Hiroshima. They knew what to look for in the city as they approached.

At 12 miles (19.3 km) out, bombardier Major Thomas Ferebee took over flying the *Enola Gay* through his bombsights. Ferebee could see his target, the T-shaped Aioi Bridge over the Ota River. Two minutes before the drop, the *Enola Gay*'s radio sent out a loud noise to notify the two escort planes to get ready. Then Ferebee motioned to the radio operator to give the final warning. A 15-second continuous tone screamed out of the radio, warning the other B-29s that the bomb would be dropped in 15 seconds.

The bomb bays opened, the tone ended, Ferebee released the bombsight focused on the target, and Little Boy fell from the plane. This pulled the arming wires, which started Little Boy's clock. The plane sprang up in the air. It was more than four short tons (3.6 metric tons) lighter.

Tibbets quickly took the plane off automatic pilot and made the 155-degree diving turn to get as far away from the falling bomb as possible. A brilliant light filled the plane and the first shock wave hit. Navigator Theodore Van Kirk said, "The plane bounced, it jumped and there was a noise like a piece of sheet metal snapping."[3] Then the second shock wave hit. They circled back around to witness the destruction.

THE EXPLOSION

Little Boy fell nose down for 43 seconds. At 8:16 a.m., the two pieces of uranium slammed together to explode at 1,900 feet (580 m) off the ground. Little Boy's explosive yield was equivalent to 12,500 short tons (11,340 metric tons) of TNT.[4]

The people in the observation plane, photography plane, and *Enola Gay* said there was a blinding flash and giant fireball. Then the city was like a pot of boiling black oil with smoke and debris churning into a purple and gray cloud with a red core that grew over the city. The column of smoke rose 35,000 feet (10,700 m) into the air and billowed into a mushroom cloud.

In Hiroshima, that Monday morning had begun as most other weekdays.

A mushroom-shaped cloud rose into the sky during the bombing of Hiroshima.

HIROSHIMA:
BEFORE AND AFTER

There was not only a great loss of life at Hiroshima but also a tremendous loss of property. More than 60 percent of the city was instantly destroyed. The destruction leveled homes, hospitals, schools, grocery stores, restaurants, police stations, fire stations, and businesses. Out of the 76,000 buildings in the city, 48,000 were totally destroyed.[5] Most were burned or blown down by the blast. Water, electricity, gas, and sewage facilities were also destroyed. There was no place for the wounded to go because 18 hospitals and 32 first-aid clinics were gone. And 90 percent of the medical staff had been killed or injured, too.[6]

Burn victims await medical treatment in Hiroshima on August 6, 1945.

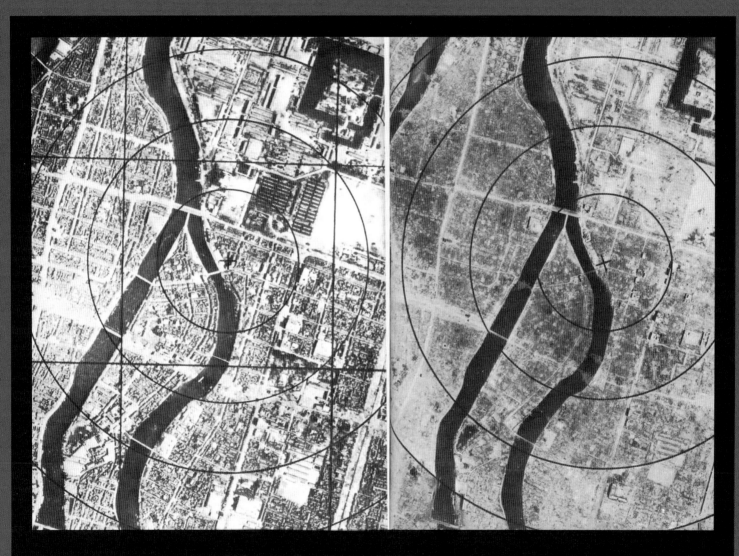

The target area of Hiroshima before the bombing, *left*, and after, *right*

Children were headed to school, businesses were opening, soldiers were exercising, and everyone was enjoying the start of a beautiful day. But everything changed suddenly as Little Boy exploded.

ON THE GROUND

Within a 0.33-mile (0.53 km) radius of Ground Zero, the heat of the fireball reached 5,400 degrees Fahrenheit (2,982°C).[7] Everything was on fire. Within a split second, anyone in the area was instantly vaporized. A man sitting on bank steps and one pulling a cart were incinerated. They left behind only their shadows burned into buildings. Close to 97 percent of the people within this area would die by the end of 1945.[8]

Those within 0.5 to two miles (0.8 to 3.2 km) from Ground Zero saw the blinding flash of light and heat. Then everything went inky black. Smoke, dust, and debris filled the air. Homes and buildings were blown over, leaving rubble burning everywhere. Nothing looked the same.

Most people's skin was burned and blistered, and their hair was singed off. What few clothes remained were charred or hung in rags. Other people lay dead

THE DEATH TOLL

Earlier in the war, the population of Hiroshima was nearly 400,000. But by August 6, the population had dropped to 280,000 to 290,000 civilians and 43,000 military personnel plus an unknown number of Korean prisoners of war.[9] Recent studies estimate the loss of life in Hiroshima by the end of 1945 was between 90,000 and 120,000.[10] But the five-year death toll reached approximately 200,000.[11] Injured people died quickly afterward. Over the next several years after the blast, radiation sickness killed more. Multiple generations of many families and entire neighborhoods were wiped out.

The atomic explosion reduced the city of Hiroshima to rubble.

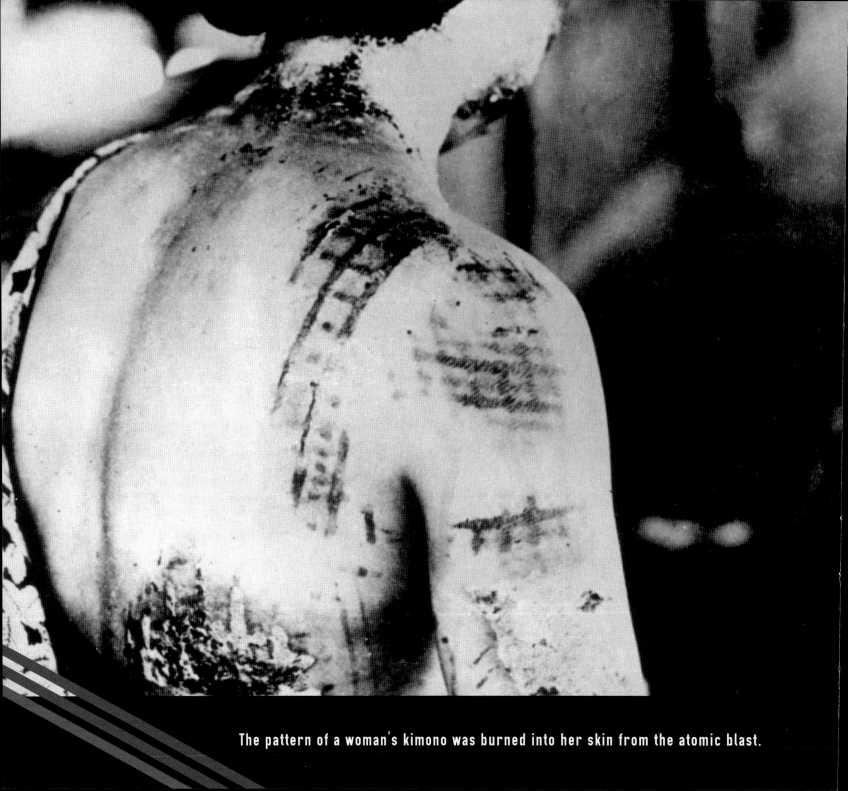

The pattern of a woman's kimono was burned into her skin from the atomic blast.

DISEASE X

Within three to four weeks after both the atomic bombings, many who survived the initial blasts began dying from an unknown illness. They became nauseous, vomited, had diarrhea, lost their appetite, got a high fever, and became weak. Then huge purplish black spots developed on their skin, they bled from their mouths, and they lost their hair. The Japanese doctors had no explanation or cure for what these seemingly healthy people were contracting. They thought it must have come from the bomb's rays, like X ray burns. So they just called it Disease X. The disease caused cancers of all kinds, and people died quickly. Those patients had radiation poisoning, also called the atomic bomb illness.

and dying where they were at the moment of the bomb's explosion. Many headed to the river or any water they could find.

Those who saw the bomb's bright flash had third-degree eye burns, leaving them totally blind. People who covered their faces with their hands saved their vision but had permanent facial burns called "the mask of Hiroshima."[12] People farther away received what looked like a severe sunburn. Some had the patterns of their clothes burned into their skin. Everyone who could move walked toward hospitals looking for help. Soon a thick, black rain began falling on Hiroshima. This rain contained radiation, which poured down on the already sick and dying.

US President Truman, *center*, met with Soviet leader Joseph Stalin, *right*, and British Prime Minister Winston Churchill, *left*, at the Potsdam Conference.

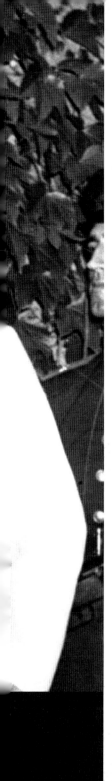

DROPPING FAT MAN

Japan's political leaders thought the Hiroshima bombing was a way to accept an unconditional surrender without shame. But the military leaders refused to surrender under any condition.

During the Potsdam Conference, the Allies tried to convince Japan to accept an unconditional surrender. This would mean their emperor would be removed from power once they surrendered. But the Japanese wanted to keep their monarchy. The United States hoped Japan would surrender before another bomb was dropped. President Truman was briefed on the Hiroshima bombing on his trip back to the United States from the Potsdam Conference, which had ended on August 2.

Soviet leader Stalin was shocked at the news of the devastation at Hiroshima. Truman had told him of the new weapon at Potsdam, but Stalin had no idea of its power. This prompted the Soviets to accelerate their plans to join the fighting against Japan by

August 9. Their 1.6 million troops were waiting on the Chinese border ready to attack occupying Japanese troops.[1] They hoped if Japan was defeated, the Soviets could gain more territory for themselves.

The US War Department wanted to inform the Japanese people about the Hiroshima bombing, in hopes they would convince their leaders to accept surrender. The Allies sent a script to Radio Saipan, a radio station in Japan, asking it to be broadcast in Japanese every 15 minutes. The broadcast described the power of the atomic bomb. It said the Japanese people should ask their leaders about what happened at Hiroshima. The broadcast asked that the Japanese try to convince their emperor to end the war, or the United States would use the atomic bomb again on Japan.

The United States decided to drop a second atomic bomb. On August 7, the commanders met to schedule the next bomb drop. Originally, the plan was to drop the Fat Man plutonium bomb on another Japanese city on August 11. But Parsons and Ramsey changed the schedule to drop on August 10. When Tibbets heard this news, he said they should move the drop date to August 9, when the weather was projected to be the best of the next five days.

ASSEMBLING FAT MAN

The pressure was on the Fat Man assembly team to put together the more complex implosion device. The scientific staff was exhausted and Ensign Bernard O'Keefe, part of the arming crew, said, "Cutting two full days would prevent us from completing a number of important checkout procedures, but orders were orders."[2]

Military engineers assembled the Fat Man bomb at the Tinian base.

Once the schedule was changed, O'Keefe started the arming process on the evening of August 7. It was his job to connect the firing unit on the bomb's front with the four radar units in the tail. Working in the air-conditioned assembly room on Tinian, he found the cable was in backward. So O'Keefe had to improvise. He disconnected the ends and soldered them correctly to keep the bomb drop schedule on track.

By 10:00 p.m. the following day, O'Keefe and the rest of the assembly crew had finished assembling the large, round Fat Man bomb. It was then loaded into the bomb bay of the B-29 *Bockscar*, named after its usual pilot, Captain Fredrick Bock. However, Major Charles Sweeney was assigned to pilot *Bockscar* for this mission.

The bomb was rechecked. Then it was armed and ready to go. It only needed its green plugs replaced with the red ones once it was in the air. At 12:01 a.m.

WRONG ENDS

On the night of August 7, O'Keefe and an army technician were completing the final Fat Man bomb connections when they found a problem. The cable that was to plug into the firing unit wouldn't fit. Someone had put the cable in backward. To fix the problem, they would have to disassemble the explosive shell, which had taken most of the day to put together. Doing this would push the bomb drop date back and they would miss the window of good weather. O'Keefe could switch the ends around, but only by using a soldering iron. But nothing that could generate heat was allowed in the Explosive Assembly Room.

O'Keefe decided to risk it. O'Keefe disconnected the cable ends, reversed them, and soldered them in place. He had to do this while keeping the hot soldering iron far away from the detonator, to prevent a major explosion.

HAREK   SGT. A. DEHART   2ND. LT. F. OLIVI   S/S. E. BUCKLEY   CPT. K. BEAHAN   MAJ. C. SWEENEY   S/S. R. GALLAGHER   CPT. J. VAN PELT   1ST LT. C.
                                                                                                PILOT

The *Bockscar* crew and their plane

on August 9, the crew was briefed on the importance of their mission. Then the members were shown detailed maps and aerial photographs of the two possible target cities, Kokura and Nagasaki, so they could memorize them. They went over the details of the mission including altitude, weather, and what to do in case of an emergency.

At 1:30 a.m., the crew ran preflight tests on the *Bockscar*. The flight engineer discovered the pumps that allowed the plane to use its reserve gas weren't working. Tibbets told Sweeney, "You don't need that gas, so there's no reason to delay this."[3]

THROUGH THE STORM

Bockscar taxied down the runway and took off from Tinian during a tropical thunderstorm. The two companion B-29 observation planes followed right behind. Ten minutes into the flight, weaponeer Navy Commander Frederick Ashworth fully armed the Fat Man bomb. This allowed Major Sweeney to pressurize the plane and cruise to 17,000 feet (5,200 m) so they would be above the storm squalls.

The three planes separated during the thunderstorm but had arranged a rendezvous over the island of Yakushima at 9:10 a.m. *Bockscar* arrived and circled the island until one of the accompanying planes—*The Great Artiste*—arrived at 9:20 a.m. The third plane never arrived, so they left without it. It was later found that *The Big Stink*, the scientific plane, had circled at 39,000 feet (11,900 m) instead of the ordered 30,000 feet (9,100 m). With radio silence and the bad storm, they didn't know they were hidden above the others.

The reports came back from the weather planes over the target cities. Kokura had low clouds and Nagasaki had increasing cloudiness. The primary target of Kokura was selected as the drop city.

The B-29 *Bockscar* carrying the armed Fat Man bomb arrived at Kokura at 10:44 a.m. to find it covered in haze and smoke. Sweeney circled around Kokura, hoping there would be an opening in the clouds so his bombardier, Captain Raymond "Kermit" Beahan, could get a visual on their target, the Kokura Arsenal. They were not allowed to use radar to help them find their target when dropping the atomic bomb. So *Bockscar* circled around two more times. But after 45 minutes, they were running low on fuel.

The Japanese started wondering why two B-29s were circling their city. They sent up fighter planes and shot at the B-29s. Since they had a live atomic bomb aboard, Sweeney and Ashworth decided that the mission should leave Kokura and fly to their second target, Nagasaki.

BOMBING NAGASAKI

With fuel running low, they could only make one pass over Nagasaki before flying

THE GREAT ARTISTE SWITCH

The Great Artiste carried the instrumentation to record the bombing at Hiroshima. It was scheduled to be the plane, piloted by Major Sweeney, to drop the second bomb on Japan on August 11. In order to do this, the ground crew was to remove all the instruments from *The Great Artiste* and install them in another support plane.

But the commanders moved the drop day up by two days, which didn't give the ground crew enough time to switch things around. So *The Great Artiste* became the support plane on the second bomb drop.

The pilots were also switched around. Sweeney ended up flying the *Bockscar* airplane carrying the Fat Man bomb and Captain Bock flew *The Great Artiste* with the recording instruments still aboard.

back to Okinawa for gas. Nagasaki was also covered in clouds. If they weren't able to visually drop the bomb, they'd have to dump it in the ocean.

Bombardier Beahan couldn't see his primary target, the Mitsubishi plant that made the torpedoes used at Pearl Harbor. Then, at the last minute, Beahan shouted, "I've got the target!"[4] He'd seen a hole in the clouds. Beahan had a 20-second visual, long enough for the computer in the bombing sight to lock in on a nearby stadium through the hole in the clouds. The warning signal went out over the radio to the other B-29, and the crews put on their goggles.

The Fat Man bomb was released August 9, 1945, at 11:02 a.m. It exploded at 1,650 feet (500 m) above Nagasaki with a force of 22,000 short tons (20,000 metric tons) of TNT.[5] The planes filled with a flash of light and were hit by several shock waves. *New York Times* writer William Laurence, in the observation

MAYDAY! MAYDAY!

Before taking off for Japan, the *Bockscar* crew knew the plane's reserve fuel pumps weren't working. So they couldn't use the gas in those tanks. After using extra gas to circle Yakushima and look for a cloud opening above Kokura, they were low on gas.

After dropping Fat Man, the plane made one circle around the mushroom cloud and went directly to Okinawa, the closest US military base. Pilot Sweeney put the plane on a long slow glide to the island. As they approached, he got on the radio and called, "Mayday! Mayday!" to summon help.[6] But there was no response. Running on fumes, Sweeney called the tower and said, "We're going to land!"[7] They later found the *Bockscar* had only 35 gallons (132.5 L) of gas left. For a giant B-29 Superfortress, they were basically out of gas.

The atomic mushroom cloud billowed over Nagasaki.

plane, said, "Each [explosion was] resounding like the boom of cannon fire hitting our plane from all directions."[8]

Nagasaki's mushroom cloud rose to 45,000 feet (13,700 m). But not as much damage occurred at Nagasaki as at Hiroshima. Steep hills surrounded the city, which helped confine the explosion. The bomb caused less damage to property and resulted in fewer fatalities than Hiroshima. Factories were destroyed, but the downtown area where most civilians lived received little damage. In total, 44 percent of the city was destroyed.[9]

The population of Nagasaki on August 9 was approximately 280,000 people. Recent studies estimate that by the end of 1945, the fatalities in Nagasaki were between 60,000 and 80,000.[10] Within five years, approximately 140,000 people died, which was 54 percent of the city's population.[11]

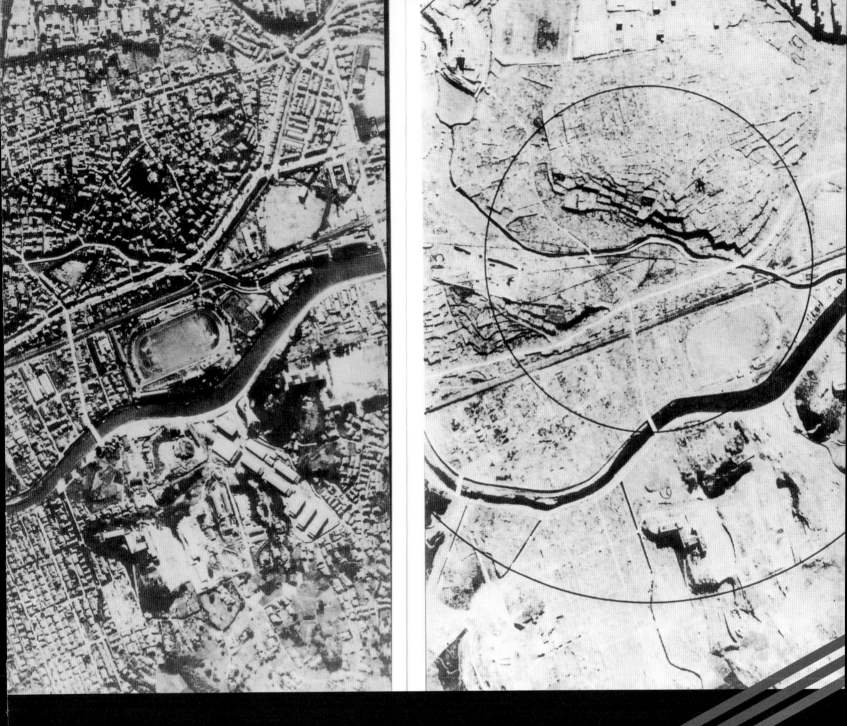

An aerial view shows Nagasaki before the explosion, *left*, and after, *right*.

A Japanese official signs the formal unconditional surrender papers for Japan.

A NEW ATOMIC WORLD

Both bombs had been dropped, and hundreds of thousands of Japanese citizens were dead. Still, the Japanese refused to surrender to the Allies. But on August 10, Emperor Hirohito sent a message to the United States. Japan would accept the Potsdam Declaration of surrender, as long as he would remain as ruler.

Truman and his military leaders could not accept a conditional Japanese surrender, an agreement under which Japan would be able to set some of the terms. Until Japan's unconditional surrender, the United States was going to keep dropping incendiary bombs. On August 10, 114 B-29s dropped incendiary bombs on Japan.[1] On August 13, 1,014 planes dropped more than 12 million pounds (5.4 million kg) of high explosives and incendiary bombs on several Japanese cities.[2] On August 14, B-29s dropped leaflets on Tokyo stating in Japanese that Japan's leaders needed to sign the surrender.

Finally, a message of Japan's full acceptance of the Potsdam Declaration reached Washington, DC, on August 14. President Truman immediately announced the news from the White House. Once people in the United States heard the news, bells rang, horns blared, and they danced in the streets. Truman said to a crowd around the White House, "This is a great day—the day we have been waiting for."[3]

On August 15, Emperor Hirohito made his first ever public radio speech, saying that because of the enemy's use of "a new and most cruel bomb" Japan unconditionally surrendered.[4] At 9:00 a.m. on September 2, the formal surrender took place on the USS *Missouri*, anchored in Tokyo Bay. Eleven Japanese delegates signed the Japanese Instrument of Surrender agreement followed by US Navy Admiral Chester Nimitz and Army General Douglas MacArthur and the generals and admirals of the nine other Allied nations. The Allied representatives

COUP ATTEMPT

On August 14, Emperor Hirohito recorded his first speech of Japan's surrender on a gramophone, at the Japanese Broadcasting Corporation. The record was hidden because there was so much controversy over Japan's surrender.

Several Japanese military leaders didn't think Japan should surrender. At 11:30 p.m., more than 1,000 soldiers and Imperial Guards led by Major Kenji Hatanaka and Colonel Masataka Ida began a coup. They surrounded the emperor's palace grounds, cut the telephone lines, and searched unsuccessfully for the recording.

They killed two Imperial Guard commanders, burned down two cabinet members' homes, and dropped leaflets over Tokyo saying, "We will continue the war. The Imperial Rescript is a forgery."[5] Army General Shizuichi Tanaka, who was in charge of all troops, arrived at the emperor's palace and ordered them to disband.

Crowds filled New York City's Times Square celebrating the Japanese surrender.

were from the United Kingdom, France, the Netherlands, Canada, China, the Soviet Union, Australia, and New Zealand. General MacArthur then said, "Today the guns are silent. A great tragedy has ended. A great victory has been won. . . . The entire world is quietly at peace."[6]

BLOOD ON MY HANDS

Oppenheimer became a celebrity, and the press dubbed him "the Father of the Atomic Bomb."[7] On August 30, Los Alamos scientists wrote and signed "The Document," which was sent to Washington, DC. It pointed out the dangers of an arms race, the impossibility of defending against an atomic bomb, and the need for international control of atomic weapons.

Oppenheimer retired as director of Los Alamos on October 16, 1945. At his farewell ceremony, he said, "Today . . . pride must be tempered with a profound concern. If atomic bombs are to be added as new weapons to the arsenals of a warring world, or to the arsenals of nations preparing for war, then the time will come when mankind will curse the names of Los Alamos and Hiroshima."[8]

On October 25, Oppenheimer met with President Truman to talk about the spread of atomic weapons. Truman asked Oppenheimer when he thought the Soviets could build a bomb, but Oppenheimer couldn't guess. Truman believed the Soviets could never build a bomb. Oppenheimer felt Truman didn't understand the problem and said, "Mr. President, I feel I have blood on my hands."[9] Truman stood to signal the end of the meeting and said, "Don't worry; we're going to work something out."[10] But after Oppenheimer left, Truman muttered, "Blood on his hands, dammit, he hasn't half as much blood on his hands as I have. You just don't go around bellyaching about it."[11] Even

Oppenheimer testified before the Senate Military Affairs Committee on October 17, 1945.

JAPAN'S RECONSTRUCTION

General MacArthur headed the reconstruction of Japan after World War II, from 1945 to 1952. The Allies occupied Japan to dismantle their military, stabilize their economy, and begin social reforms.

The Supreme Command of Allied Powers introduced land reform to help small farmers get out from under rich landowners' power. They tried to break up business monopolies to convert the economy into a free market system. They also worked to give greater rights to women.

The weakened Japanese economy was given a boost during the Korean War in the 1950s. Japan became the principal supply depot for the United Nations (UN) forces. The United States still maintains bases on Okinawa and at other locations in Japan.

though Oppenheimer helped build the atomic bombs, it was Truman's ultimate responsibility for dropping them on Japan.

PUBLIC OPINION

By the end of August 1945, 85 percent of Americans approved using atomic bombs to end the war.[12] But over time, as more information was released on the devastation the bombs caused to people and property, the public's approval dropped. Debates still rage over whether it was justified to use the atomic bombs.

Those in favor of Truman's decision to use the bombs say it saved hundreds of thousands of American and Japanese lives. The Allies were scheduled to invade Japan on November 1, 1945, and there would have been massive casualties fighting on Japan's mainland and islands.

Many people believed the United States could have won the war against Japan without using the atomic bombs. Japan was close to surrender. Its navy was mostly sunk, its air force was depleted, its supply lines were cut off, and its fuel was almost gone. And the Soviet attack in China weakened Japan's forces. Approximately 1.6 million Soviet army soldiers attacked Japanese troops

Two years after the bombing, Hiroshima was 65 percent rebuilt.

occupying Manchuria in China.[13] Japan's troops were spread too thin and they had no allies to help them. Over the next two weeks, 84,000 Japanese and 12,000 Soviet soldiers died. The Soviets ended up just 30 miles (48 km) from Japan's northern island of Hokkaido.[14]

Allied military leaders believed the continued bombings and blockades could have ended the war. General Curtis LeMay believed his bombers could destroy every Japanese city by November 1. He thought Japanese leaders would soon surrender. As early as July 12, Japan was near surrender except for one sticking point, the retention of the emperor. If the United States had accepted a conditional surrender, the atomic bombs would likely not have been used.

Why did the United States drop the atomic bombs? Army leaders had planned an invasion of the Japanese home islands, but knew that there would be significant loss of life. Navy leaders were prepared to impose a blockade, but it would have taken time before it was successful. Diplomatic leaders believed if the United States agreed to allow the Japanese to retain their emperor, they would surrender. Some Americans, particularly after the Japanese attack on Pearl Harbor, were unwilling to make that commitment. In the end, the United States dropped the bombs because, from the very start of the Manhattan Project, they were weapons of war built for the purpose of using them on the enemy. The only real question was what the targets should be.

ARMS RACE

In 1945, Oppenheimer knew physicists could design even more powerful nuclear bombs. Other countries would soon build atomic bombs, which could be used against the United States. He knew the Soviets would likely build an atomic

VICTIMS' DISEASES

Hundreds of thousands were killed or injured from the two atomic bombings. In addition to the city's inhabitants, there were military personnel, Korean forced laborers, and prisoners of war. They were exposed to residual radiation from the soil, air, water, and building debris. Many contracted diseases, depending on the duration of their stays in the bombed cities.

Those who died immediately died from burns, thermal blasts, radiation, or being crushed. Victims with high radiation doses usually died within three weeks. Others contracted various illnesses such as eye diseases, blood disorders, tumors, and numerous types of cancer. There was a 30 times higher incidence of leukemia among atomic bomb survivors than unexposed Japanese.[16] Women who were pregnant when the bombs exploded had an increased chance of having babies with a smaller head size. Many babies were intellectually disabled.

bomb. Oppenheimer said in 1948, "Our atomic monopoly is like a cake of ice melting in the sun."[15]

Oppenheimer was right. On August 29, 1949, the Soviets tested their first atomic bomb in Kazakhstan (then part of the Soviet Union). It was a close copy of the Fat Man bomb. Soviet spies had obtained US bomb plans. Truman, the US military, and political leaders were shocked. Their response was to build an even more destructive bomb.

The United States and the Soviets entered an arms race beginning the Cold War, which lasted from 1945 to 1991. Truman wanted to build a bigger bomb, to keep one step ahead of the Soviets. This new kind of bomb, a hydrogen bomb, used fusion to join atoms together instead of splitting them through fission. On November 1, 1952, the United States tested its first hydrogen bomb on a tiny South Pacific island. It exploded with the force of 10 million short tons (9 million

The United States tested its first hydrogen bomb in the Pacific over the Eniwetok Atoll, Marshall Islands, on November 1, 1952.

metric tons) of TNT, which was 500 times more powerful than the Hiroshima bomb.[17]

Less than one year later, on August 12, 1953, the Soviets tested their first hydrogen bomb in Kazakhstan. From then on, winning a nuclear war became impossible. If one nation used its nuclear bombs on an enemy, it could expect nuclear bombs to be fired back.

On March 1, 1954, the United States tested an even larger hydrogen bomb on Bikini Atoll, part of the Marshall Islands in the Pacific Ocean. Its radioactive dust spread more than 7,000 square miles (18,000 sq km), making the island uninhabitable even today. The Soviets then tested a larger hydrogen bomb on October 30, 1961. This was the largest nuclear bomb explosion in history.

Since then, atomic bombs have gotten smaller but much more accurate. Any nation with enough money and resources can build a nuclear bomb. The United Kingdom, France, China, India, Pakistan, Israel, and North Korea have atomic bombs. Iran may also soon have nuclear bombs. Since 1945, more than 125,000

SOVIET SPIES

The Allies tried keeping the Manhattan Project a secret. But some scientists became Soviet spies. Two scientists helped the Soviets: Klaus Fuchs and Ted Hall. The scientists smuggled out or made copies of top-secret documents on how the plutonium bomb was built and the scientific principles of fission. These documents were telegrammed in code to Moscow. This helped the Soviets speed up building their atomic bombs. When the code was cracked, Fuchs was arrested and imprisoned, but Hall refused to confess. The Federal Bureau of Investigation didn't want to make the decoded Soviet spy messages public during a trial, and Hall knew it. In the end, Hall outsmarted the law and remained out of prison.

nuclear warheads have been built around the world.[18] That is enough bombs to destroy all life on Earth many times over.

ATOMIC WEAPON TREATIES

In the early 1980s, the United States and the Soviet Union began negotiating treaties to reduce their number of atomic weapons. In 1991, the Soviet Union had split apart. By 2013, the arsenals of the United States and Russia were down to 16,200 total atomic bombs. Today, the United States and Russia own more than 90 percent of the world's atomic weapons.[19]

A new nuclear threat has emerged between India and Pakistan. If these two nuclear countries use 0.4 percent of the world's nuclear bombs, which would be 100 bombs, the smoke could block out the sun for up to ten years.[20] Scientists believe this nuclear winter could cause farming to collapse, leading to worldwide starvation. It would be an act of suicide for the entire planet.

The building of the atomic bomb was a technological feat that brought together military, industry, and great scientific minds to build the most destructive weapon known to mankind. The bomb's use helped end World War II, but also showed the devastation that such a weapon could inflict upon people, countries, and the environment. Use of nuclear weapons remains a threat to many countries around the world.

Iranians use their nuclear facility in Natanz to process uranium.

TIMELINE

1933

Leo Szilard theorizes about a nuclear chain reaction.

1938

In Berlin, Germany, chemists experiment with fission.

October 21, 1939

The Advisory Committee on Uranium first meets in Washington, DC.

June 1942

President Franklin Roosevelt approves the production of the atomic bomb.

April 12, 1945

President Roosevelt dies and Harry S. Truman is sworn in as president.

July 16, 1945

The first atomic bomb is tested at the Trinity site in New Mexico.

July 26, 1945

The unarmed Little Boy bomb body and uranium bullet arrive at Tinian on the USS *Indianapolis*.

July 26–28, 1945

Air Transport Command C-54 planes fly to Tinian with the uranium targets, plutonium, and Fat Man's initiator.

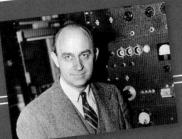

September 1942

General Leslie Groves takes over command of the Manhattan Project.

October 19, 1942

Robert Oppenheimer is hired as scientific director of the Manhattan Project.

December 2, 1942

Enrico Fermi experiments with a nuclear fission chain reaction.

March 1944

The first shipment of U-235 is sent to Los Alamos from Site X.

July 28—August 2, 1945

Three B-29s fly to Tinian, each one carrying a Fat Man bomb body.

August 6, 1945

The first atomic bomb, Little Boy, is dropped on Hiroshima, Japan.

August 9, 1945

The second atomic bomb, Fat Man, is dropped on Nagasaki, Japan.

August 14, 1945

Japan surrenders and President Truman announces the end of World War II.

ESSENTIAL FACTS

KEY PLAYERS

- J. Robert Oppenheimer is the scientist who headed the Manhattan Project.
- Leslie Groves is the military director of the Manhattan Project.
- Harry S. Truman orders the use of atomic bombs against Japan in August 1945.
- Paul W. Tibbets pilots *Enola Gay*, the bomber aircraft that drops an atomic weapon on Hiroshima, Japan.

KEY DATES

- July 16, 1945: The first US atomic bomb is tested at the Trinity site, New Mexico.
- August 6, 1945: The first atomic bomb, Little Boy, is dropped on Hiroshima, Japan.
- August 9, 1945: The second atomic bomb, Fat Man, is dropped on Nagasaki, Japan.

KEY TECHNOLOGIES

- Gun-firing uranium atomic bomb
- Implosion plutonium atomic bomb
- *Enola Gay* B-29 Superfortress

IMPACT ON THE WAR

Dropping the atomic bombs on Japan helped end World War II. The explosions destroyed Hiroshima and Nagasaki and instantly killed thousands of people. The resulting radiation continued to kill people long after the bombs were dropped.

IMPACT ON SOCIETY

Atomic bombs made future wars potentially more destructive and catastrophic than ever before. An arms race including these deadly weapons and subsequent technologies dominated much of the rest of the 1900s. People around the world worried that at any time an atomic bomb could be coming their way. During the Cold War, people built bomb shelters, schools taught students to duck and cover, and everyone hoped the devastation of an atomic bomb explosion would never happen again. Since these bombs exist, nuclear war remains a threat.

QUOTE

"An atomic chain reaction may be compared to the burning of a rubbish pile from spontaneous combustion. In such a fire, minute parts of the pile start to burn and in turn ignite other tiny fragments. When sufficient numbers of these fractional parts are heated to the kindling points, the entire heap bursts into flames."

—*Enrico Fermi*

GLOSSARY

ARSENAL

A place where arms and ammunition are made and stored.

ARTILLERY

Large guns or missile launchers, as distinguished from small arms; also, the troops or branch of the military that uses these weapons.

BOMBARDIER

A bomber aircraft crew member who controls the aircraft and releases bombs while over the target area.

CASUALTY

A person who is injured, missing, or killed during a military campaign.

COUP

An attempt to overthrow leaders.

FISSION

The splitting of an atom to release energy.

FLAK

Antiaircraft fire.

IMPLOSION

A blast inward toward a core.

INCENDIARY
A weapon used to start fires.

MAYDAY
An international signal used as a distress call for help.

NEUTRON
A small particle of matter that's part of the nucleus of all atoms, except the hydrogen atom.

PLUTONIUM
A radioactive element used to make nuclear weapons, similar to uranium.

RADIATION
A form of energy that can damage living tissue.

RADIOACTIVE FALLOUT
Particles containing toxic radiation that fall to the ground after a nuclear explosion.

TNT
A very powerful explosive.

URANIUM
A radioactive element used to make nuclear weapons, similar to plutonium.

ADDITIONAL RESOURCES

SELECTED BIBLIOGRAPHY

Bird, Kai, and Martin J. Sherwin. *American Prometheus: The Triumph and Tragedy of J. Robert Oppenheimer.* New York: Knopf, 2005. Print.

Kelly, Cynthia C. *The Manhattan Project: The Birth of the Atomic Bomb in the Words of Its Creators, Eyewitnesses, and Historians.* New York: Black Dog & Leventhal, 2007. Print.

Rhodes, Richard. *The Making of the Atomic Bomb.* New York: Simon, 1986. Print.

Szasz, Ferenc Morton. *The Day the Sun Rose Twice: The Story of the Trinity Site Nuclear Explosion, July 16, 1945.* Albuquerque: U of New Mexico P, 1984. Print.

Winkler, Allan M. *Life under a Cloud: American Anxiety about the Atom.* New York: Oxford UP, 1993. Print.

FURTHER READINGS

Fetter-Vorm, Jonathan. *Trinity: A Graphic History of the First Atomic Bomb.* New York: Hill and Wang, 2012. Print.

Vander Hook, Sue. *Manhattan Project.* Minneapolis, MN: Abdo, 2011. Print.

WEBSITES

To learn more about Essential Library of World War II, visit **booklinks.abdopublishing.com**. These links are routinely monitored and updated to provide the most current information available.

PLACES TO VISIT

Bradbury Science Museum
Los Alamos National Laboratory
1350 Central Avenue
Los Alamos, NM 87544
505-667-7000
http://www.lanl.gov/museum/index.shtml
Based in Los Alamos, New Mexico, this museum is home to 40 interactive exhibits in three galleries: History, Defense, and Research. Exhibits include replicas of the Little Boy and Fat Man bombs, movies, plutonium, and more.

Hiroshima Peace Memorial Museum
1-2 Nakajimama-cho, Naka-ku
Hiroshima City, Japan 730-0811
+81-82-241-4004
http://www.pcf.city.hiroshima.jp/index_e2.html
Based in Hiroshima, Japan, this museum contains artifacts, survivor accounts, and the Kids' Peace Plaza.

SOURCE NOTES

CHAPTER 1. THE TRINITY TEST

1. Steve Sheinkin. *Bomb: The Race to Build and Steal the World's Most Dangerous Weapon*. New York: Roaring Brook, 2012. Print. 180.

2. Richard Rhodes. *The Making of the Atomic Bomb*. New York: Simon, 1986. Print. 652.

3. Ibid. 653.

4. Steve Sheinkin. *Bomb: The Race to Build and Steal the World's Most Dangerous Weapon*. New York: Roaring Brook, 2012. Print. 178.

5. Richard Rhodes. *The Making of the Atomic Bomb*. New York: Simon, 1986. Print. 656–657.

CHAPTER 2. BUILDING THE BOMBS

1. Richard Rhodes. *The Making of the Atomic Bomb*. New York: Simon, 1986. Print. 314.

2. Ibid. 317.

3. Denise Kiernan. *The Girls of Atomic City*. New York: Touchstone, 2013. Print. 100.

4. Kai Bird and Martin J. Sherwin. *American Prometheus: The Triumph and Tragedy of J. Robert Oppenheimer*. New York: Knopf, 2005. Print. 185.

5. US Department of Energy. "Fermi's Own Story." *The First Reactor*. Washington, DC: United States Department of Energy, 1982. Print. 22–23.

6. Denise Kiernan. *The Girls of Atomic City*. New York: Touchstone, 2013. Print. 102–104.

7. Steve Sheinkin. *Bomb: The Race to Build and Steal the World's Most Dangerous Weapon*. New York: Roaring Brook Press, 2012. Print. 96.

CHAPTER 3. TESTING THE BOMB

1. Richard Rhodes. *The Making of the Atomic Bomb*. New York: Simon, 1986. Print. 675.

2. Steve Sheinkin. *Bomb: The Race to Build and Steal the World's Most Dangerous Weapon*. New York: Roaring Brook, 2012. Print. 183.

3. Kai Bird and Martin J. Sherwin. "Building the Bomb." *Smithsonian*. Aug. 2005. Print. 88–96.

4. Richard Rhodes. *The Making of the Atomic Bomb*. New York: Simon, 1986. Print. 677.

5. Ferenc Morton Szasz. *The Day the Sun Rose Twice: The Story of the Trinity Site Nuclear Explosion, July 16, 1945*. Albuquerque: U of New Mexico P, 1984. Print. 86–87.

6. Denise Kiernan. *The Girls of Atomic City*. New York: Touchstone, 2013. Print. 237.

7. *Where the Buck Stops: The Personal and Private Writing of Harry S. Truman.* Ed. Margaret Truman. New York: Warner, 1989. Print. 205.

8. Denise Kiernan. *The Girls of Atomic City.* New York: Touchstone, 2013. Print. 238.

9. Richard Rhodes. *The Making of the Atomic Bomb.* New York: Simon, 1986. Print. 650–651.

10. *Where the Buck Stops: The Personal and Private Writing of Harry S. Truman.* Ed. Margaret Truman. New York: Warner, 1989. Print. 204.

CHAPTER 4. TRAINING AND TARGETS

1. Richard Rhodes. *The Making of the Atomic Bomb.* New York: Simon, 1986. Print. 585.

2. C. Peter Chen. "Battle of Iwo Jima." *World War II Database.* Lava Development, n.d. Web. 30 Mar. 2015.

3. Richard Rhodes. *The Making of the Atomic Bomb.* New York: Simon, 1986. Print. 580.

4. Ibid. 680–681.

5. Ibid. 627–628.

6. Alonzo L. Hamby. "Truman and the Bomb." *History Today.* Aug. 1995. Print. 18–25.

7. Ferenc Morton Szasz. *The Day the Sun Rose Twice: The Story of the Trinity Site Nuclear Explosion, July 16, 1945.* Albuquerque: U of New Mexico P, 1984. Print. 154.

CHAPTER 5. TRANSPORTING THE BOMBS

1. Dan Kurzman. *Fatal Voyage: The Sinking of the USS Indianapolis.* New York: Crown, 2008. Print. 37.

2. "The Story: Torpedoed Ship." *U.S.S. Indianapolis.* Netwide Development, n.d. Web. 30 Mar. 2015.

3. Ibid.

4. "Little Boy and Fat Man." *Atomic Heritage Foundation.* Atomic Heritage Foundation, n.d. Web. 30 Mar. 2015.

5. "Lt. William A King—Nagasaki Bomb Core Courier to Tinian Island." *Manhattan Project Heritage Preservation Association.* Manhattan Project Heritage Preservation Association, 2005. Web. 30 Mar. 2015.

CHAPTER 6. DROPPING LITTLE BOY

1. Bill Gilbert. *Air Power: Heroes and Heroism in American Flight Missions, 1916 to Today.* New York: Citadel, 2003. Print. 146–147.

2. Richard Rhodes. *The Making of the Atomic Bomb.* New York: Simon, 1986. Print. 708.

3. Ibid. 710.

4. Ibid. 711.

5. Ibid. 728–730.

6. Ibid.

SOURCE NOTES
CONTINUED

7. Cynthia C. Kelly. *The Manhattan Project: The Birth of the Atomic Bomb in the Words of Its Creators, Eyewitnesses, and Historians.* New York: Black Dog & Leventhal, 2007. Print. 331.

8. Frank Barnaby. "The Continuing Body Count at Hiroshima and Nagasaki." *Bulletin of the Atomic Scientists.* Dec. 1977. Print. 51.

9. Richard Rhodes. *The Making of the Atomic Bomb.* New York: Simon, 1986. Print. 713.

10. David Richardson. "Lessons from Hiroshima and Nagasaki: The Most Exposed and Most Vulnerable." *Bulletin of the Atomic Scientists.* May 2012. Print. 29.

11. Richard Rhodes. *The Making of the Atomic Bomb.* New York: Simon, 1986. Print. 734.

12. Ibid. 715–716.

CHAPTER 7. DROPPING FAT MAN

1. Richard Rhodes. *The Making of the Atomic Bomb.* New York: Simon, 1986. Print. 736.

2. Ibid. 738.

3. Coco Masters, Carolina A. Miranda, and Tim Padgett. "The Men Who Dropped the Bombs." *Time.* 1 Aug. 2005. Print. 46–48.

4. Ibid.

5. Cynthia C. Kelly. *The Manhattan Project: The Birth of the Atomic Bomb in the Words of Its Creators, Eyewitnesses, and Historians.* New York: Black Dog & Leventhal, 2007. Print. 350–351.

6. Coco Masters, Carolina A. Miranda, and Tim Padgett. "The Men Who Dropped the Bombs." *Time.* 1 Aug. 2005. Print. 46–48.

7. Ibid.

8. Cynthia C. Kelly. *The Manhattan Project: The Birth of the Atomic Bomb in the Words of Its Creators, Eyewitnesses, and Historians.* New York: Black Dog & Leventhal, 2007. Print. 350–351.

9. Dennis D. Wainstock. *The Decision to Drop the Atomic Bomb: Hiroshima and Nagasaki: August 1945.* New York: Enigma, 2013. Print. 92.

10. David Richardson. "Lessons from Hiroshima and Nagasaki: The Most Exposed and Most Vulnerable." *Bulletin of the Atomic Scientists.* May 2012. Print. 29.

11. Richard Rhodes. *The Making of the Atomic Bomb.* New York: Simon, 1986. Print. 742.

12. Norman F. Ramsey. "August 1945: The B-29 Flight Logs." *Bulletin of the Atomic Scientists.* Dec.1982. Print. 35.

CHAPTER 8. A NEW ATOMIC WORLD

1. J. Robert Moskin. *Mr. Truman's War, the Final Victories of World War II and the Birth of the Postwar World.* New York: Random House, 1996. Print. 316.

2. Ibid.

3. Ibid. 319.

4. Richard Rhodes. *The Making of the Atomic Bomb.* New York: Simon, 1986. Print. 743–745.

5. Dennis D. Wainstock. *The Decision to Drop the Atomic Bomb: Hiroshima and Nagasaki: August 1945.* New York: Enigma Books, Print. 201–203.

6. J. Robert. Moskin. *Mr. Truman's War, the Final Victories of World War II and the Birth of the Postwar World.* New York: Random House, 1996. Print. 338-9.

7. Kai Bird and Martin J. Sherwin. "Building the Bomb." *Smithsonian.* Aug. 2005. Print. 88–96.

8. Kai Bird and Martin J. Sherwin. *American Prometheus: The Triumph and Tragedy of J. Robert Oppenheimer.* New York: Alfred A. Knopf, 2005. Print. 323–329.

9. Ibid. 331–332.

10. Ibid.

11. Ibid.

12. Cynthia C. Kelly. *The Manhattan Project: The Birth of the Atomic Bomb in the Words of Its Creators, Eyewitnesses, and Historians.* New York: Black Dog & Leventhal, 2007. Print. 407.

13. Richard Rhodes. *The Making of the Atomic Bomb.* New York: Simon, 1986. Print. 736.

14. Associated Press. "Historians: Soviet Offensive, Key to Japan's WWII Surrender Was Eclipsed by the A-bombs." *FOX News.* FOX News Network, LLC. 14 Aug. 2010. Web. 30 Mar. 2015.

15. Steve Sheinkin. *Bomb: The Race to Build and Steal the World's Most Dangerous Weapon.* New York: Roaring Brook Press, 2012. Print. 220.

16. Frank Barnaby. "The Continuing Body Count at Hiroshima and Nagasaki." *Bulletin of the Atomic Scientists.* Dec. 1977. Print. 50.

17. Steve Sheinkin. *Bomb: The Race to Build and Steal the World's Most Dangerous Weapon.* New York: Roaring Brook, 2012. Print. 233–235.

18. Hans M. Kristensen and Robert S. Norris. "Global Nuclear Weapons Inventories, 1945–2013." *Bulletin of the Atomic Scientists.* Sept. 2013. Print. 75.

19. Ibid.

20. Alan Robock and Owen B. Toon. "Local Nuclear War, Global Suffering." *Scientific American.* Jan. 2010. Print. 74–81.

INDEX

ABOUT THE AUTHOR

Mary Meinking is a graphic designer and writer. She's written more than 30 nonfiction books and has been published in a dozen different children's magazines. She has written about history, arts and crafts, extreme jobs, animals, pop stars, and travel. When not working, writing, or hanging out with her family in Iowa, Meinking enjoys doing arts and crafts, baking, gardening, and traveling.

ABOUT THE CONSULTANT

Allan M. Winkler is a distinguished professor of history at Miami University in Ohio. He has also taught at Yale University, the University of Oregon, the University of Helsinki in Finland, the University of Amsterdam in the Netherlands, and the University of Nairobi in Kenya. Winkler is a prize-winning teacher and author of eight books, which include: *The Politics of Propaganda: The Office of War Information, 1942–1945*; *Home Front U.S.A.: America during World War II*; *Franklin D. Roosevelt and the Making of Modern America*; *Life Under a Cloud: American Anxiety about the Atom*; and *"To Everything There Is a Season": Pete Seeger and the Power of Song*. Winkler is also a coauthor of the college textbook *The American People: Creating a Nation and a Society* and the high school textbook *America: Pathways to the Present*.

10/3/17